Gongs and Tam-Tams –

A Guide for Percussionists, Drummers
and Sound Healers

Gongs and Tam-Tams –

A Guide for Percussionists, Drummers and Sound Healers

Phil McNamara

Published by Philip McNamara

All photographs by the author unless otherwise state. The author would particularly like to thank Paiste for their co-operation in allowing the gong manufacturing process at the Schacht-Audorf factory to be photographed

A CIP catalogue record for this book is available from the British Library.

ISBN 978-0-9573326-0-7

Book and cover design by Clare Brayshaw

This edition printed by ImprintDigital.com

CONTENTS

ACKNOWLEDGEMENTS

The writing of any book involves a lot of research and the help and co-operation of a number of people. In particular, I would like to register my appreciation and thanks to the following persons who took the trouble to discuss aspects of their work, allowed me to check the accuracy of what I had written or gave constructive feedback when reviewing the book's content:-

At Paiste:	Jorg Kohlmorgen, Sven Meier. Also Dirk Jurgensen
At Oetken Gongs:	Broder and Ines Oetken
At Zildjian:	John Sorenson
At Sabian:	Peter Stairs
At SONA:	Johannes Heimrath
The Independent: Gong Makers	Steve Hubback, Walter Meyer, Matt Nolan, Michael Paiste
The Suppliers:	Julian Marsden at Ecymbals (Paiste products), Kevin Smith at the Cymbal Centre (UFIP products) Ed Mann (UFIP Gongs USA)
The Sound Healers:	Sheila Whittaker, Don Conreaux, Pauline McCrann
The Players:	Graham Johns, Andrea Centazzo

And last, but by no means least, to my wife Karen who has 'tolerated' my obsession with gongs and proof read and corrected the text and saved it from my north of England grammar, all whilst looking after our baby son Connor!

INTRODUCTION

M y own interest in gongs (or more specifically 'tam-tams') extends back nearly forty years to a time when I was finding my own likes and dislikes in classical music and developing an interest in the large symphonic works of the late 19th Century as well as British, American and Russian composers of the 20th Century. One percussion instrument caught my ear, often being used at dramatic moments in the music to underpin a climax, round off a passage or section of the score, or quietly add to a brooding atmosphere. Reading of the scores revealed this instrument to be a 'tam-tam' though some scores referred to it as a 'gong'. Curiously, some scores had more than one, being referred to as gongs and tam-tams in the same piece! Also, different orchestras had different sounding tam-tams, often dependant on what part of the world the orchestra came from. This prompted many questions in my mind and eventually I figured out the answers, but there was no one book (and web sites had not been invented back then) that I could go to which would have satisfied my curiosity.

I played my first tam-tam when I was 19, a 20"/51cm Paiste Symphonic Gong in a music shop in Leeds. I desperately wanted to buy this but, as a student, I couldn't afford it or justify it apart from just wanting to have one! I poured over the Paiste catalogue wondering what on earth a 60"/152cm Symphonic Gong sounded like and which ones I would buy given the money (something I'm still doing to this day!). I played my first large tam-tam at a concert given by the Royal Liverpool Philharmonic Orchestra when I was 20, boldly striding up onto the stage after the concert and asking if I could have a go and being handed a beater by a somewhat perplexed looking percussionist! Playing your first large tam-tam is an experience not easily forgotten.

In 1985 I purchased my first tam-tam, a 32"/81cm Paiste Symphonic Gong from a shop in Liverpool. Strangely, although the name of the shop has changed twice in the intervening years, I now get all my Paiste gongs from this shop, now named ADC Drums (www.ecymbals.co.uk). The proprietor Julian Marsden arranged for me to visit the Paiste factory during the writing of this book, fulfilling a long held ambition. I have since bought and sold two other 32"/81cm Symphonic Gongs and added a 38"/96cm Symphonic Gong from the Royal Liverpool Philharmonic in 1994. A couple of years later a 24"/60cm Chao gong followed and over the millennium, a 40"/102cm Zildjian Chao Gong was added.

My gong journey really moved into top gear two years ago with the discovery that gongs are being used for healing purposes. Since the discovery of this most pleasing use of gongs, my collection of gongs has multiplied, I have met many influential and famous people in the worlds of gong playing, healing, manufacture and sales and it has given me the inspiration to write this book. Nothing like this book (which focuses just on gongs and tam-tams) has existed before, though I am aware of at least one other book being written as I write this. Other books on music or percussion instruments include sections on gongs and tam-tams though not in any real detail. There are plenty of websites around which talk about these instruments, though they often quote similar sources, make one or two common mistakes, or perpetuate one or two myths. This book in part attempts to correct these inaccuracies, but its main aim is to provide the reader with a one-stop shop covering all aspects of the gong including:

- construction
- history
- playing techniques
- the paraphernalia needed in terms of beaters, cases and stands,
- cleaning and care
- and a comprehensive (but I must stress not complete) listing and description of many of the gongs available today or in the recent past.

It is intended for anyone interested in gongs, though composers, music arrangers and students of music, metallurgy and percussion history may learn something from its pages. It is merely a guide – there are many things I would like to have added to this book, such as a more in-depth study of South East Asian gongs, the manufacture of gamelan gongs and a visit to the Italian and Chinese gong factories, but present circumstances prevent me from doing this. But I'm already sketching out the second edition which I hope will also include feedback from yourselves, the readers, on gongs I have not covered, or data and information that you think would be useful to the gong community.

I hope you find it as interesting to read as I have found it to write.

The Author standing next to the World's largest commercially available gong – the Paiste 80"/203cm Symphonic Gong

In writing this book, I have used a number of musical terms to describe dynamics when playing the gong. Many people may not be familiar with these terms so a translation is provided here:

Pianissimo (pp)	very quietly
Piano (p)	quietly
Mezzo piano (mp)	reasonably quiet
Mezzo forte (mf)	reasonably loud
Forte (f)	loud
Fortissimo (ff)	very loud
Fortississimo (fff)	very, very loud

ABOUT THE AUTHOR

Phil McNamara was born in Burnley, Lancashire in 1962. A lifelong interest in gongs and tam-tams developed from an early age whilst listening to classical music and attending concerts by the Halle and Royal Liverpool Philharmonic Orchestras. Whilst at college in Sheffield studying Chemistry, he began learning percussion in the local polytechnic orchestra. Mainly self taught, he has played percussion in a number of local orchestras in Lancashire, Kent, Cleveland and Yorkshire. He currently plays percussion in several orchestras in Worcestershire and Gloucestershire.

Phil purchased his first gong in 1985 and had collected several by 1999. In 2010 he discovered a new use for gongs – healing, using the

sonorous properties of the gong. He studied Sound Healing with gongs with Sheila Whittaker and the College of Sound Healing, graduating as a Gong Practitioner in 2011. His current collect of gongs has grown considerably and includes examples from different manufacturers as well as discontinued, but still sought after ranges from the Paiste company.

Phil currently livers near the Malvern Hills in Worcestershire with his wife and young son.

1. THE SOUND AND EFFECT OF THE GONG

The gong. One of the most (if not the most) powerful instruments known to humankind. Powerful, not just in terms of their sheer size and loudness, but in their ability to connect with our core self, to heal and to connect or communicate (according to some civilisations) to other dimensions, even to gods and other deities themselves. According to Yogi Bhajan, credited by many in bringing the healing power of the gong to the West in the middle of the last century, "The gong is the sound of Creativity itself. One who plays the gong plays the Universe. Out of it came all music, all sounds and all words. The sound of the gong is the nucleus of the World." Indeed, the sound of the word 'gong' closely reflects the sound 'OM' or 'AUM', the fundamental sound of the Universe.

As a percussionist, I am, along with my colleagues, often jokingly referred to as 'the noisy ones at the back of the orchestra' or the 'kitchen department' by both public and other players alike. But it never ceases to amaze me that when there is a loud crash on a large tam-tam in an orchestra, 95% of the audience will be smiling. The sound of the gong affects us all, mostly in a pleasurable way unless it is played badly or too loudly (especially if you experience 'white noise'). You can feel a pull in your stomach and an overall feeling or shiver of excitement around your body. Even their physical appearance can be pleasing. They are good to look at, can be tactile and just invite you to play them. Standing in front of a large gong has been said by some to be like standing in the presence of God. Certainly, the urge to thwack it just like the man on the Rank Organisation's trademark seems to disappear and much gentler strokes ensue.

The gong has a sound structure unlike any other instrument. Instruments that are struck or plucked have a primary note which sounds immediately then decays away quite quickly. There are a few overtones associated with the note and the sound envelope but this is small and predictable. The gong, and in particular the type of gong known in percussion circles as a 'tam-tam', has a completely different sound envelope. After the strike by the beater there is an initial tone at a certain volume. The sound then *grows* in volume and complexity. Many tones and overtones are produced encompassing many frequencies, reaching a climax before decaying away over a period of up to several minutes. Repeated beating of the gong produces wave upon wave of tones, sounds and frequencies, some building on each other, others cancelling each other out, taking the listener on a sound journey quite unlike anything else. Many people can hear other sounds within the gong – peels of bells, monks chanting or choirs of angels! It is also this complex structure of frequencies washing (or bathing – hence 'gong bath' – see later) the body that causes healing of our cells and DNA, re-aligning the cellular vibrations to their optimum

A fine collection of Paiste Symphonic, Planet and Sound Creation Gongs.

frequency by a process known as 'entrainment'. The gong has a long history of use as a musical instrument, at ceremonies, as a call for dinner or as a warning device. But it is the use of the gong as a healing instrument that in recent years has brought it more into our everyday lives.

I have already referred to 'gongs' and 'tam-tams' and quite easily use either term freely within the text of this book. So, before we look at the history of the gong, it is worth trying to define a gong and a tam-tam.

2.   GONG OR TAM-TAM?

This is one of the most common questions asked about the family of instruments known as gongs. Most of the time, the general public use the term gong to describe any of the instruments found in this family without another thought. The word gong has its origins in Java where it refers to a particular instrument (bonang) in a gamelan orchestra but its meaning has changed over time to describe any circular metallic percussion instruments from the Far East.

For musicians (mainly percussionists) and composers, the term tam-tam describes a very specific member of the gong family. Most of the gongs seen in orchestras, wind bands, brass bands and rock bands are, in fact, tam-tams. To the majority of percussionists, a gong is an instrument that is tuned to a particular pitch and tends to be smaller in diameter than a tam-tam.

Tam-tam is commonly used, regardless of the nationality of the composer, to describe an instrument that is usually of large diameter (28"/71cm – 40"/102cm) that produces a large splash of sound when struck *forte* or *fortissimo*. However, it is still worth noting that some English composers, especially those composing between the late-1800s and mid-1950s use the term 'gong' when, in fact, a tam-tam is required. Gustav Holst, Havergal Brian and Benjamin Britten are particular culprits in this respect. Vaughan Williams was somewhat more enlightened and uses both terms. His Symphony No. 8 for instance uses tuned gongs of a specific pitch and his symphonies No.2 and No.7 use a tam-tam (to very good effect).

Given that, until recently, percussionists in the West were the people who routinely came into contact with these instruments it is not surprising that the word tam-tam came into routine use in gong terminology. Over the past ten years however, there has been a surge of interest in using the gong's healing and mystical powers in sound healing therapy, yoga, alternative medicine and 'New Age' spiritualism. Sound healers and therapists may wonder what all the fuss is about. The instruments they use are generically referred to as gongs but are more often referred to by the manufacturers' description e.g. Paiste Planet Gong 'Mars'.

To help clarify some of these issues and for the purposes of this book I have made the following distinctions:-

GONG

This is the generic name for the family of percussion instruments (excluding cymbals) that are usually circular, or a disk when looked at in plan form, made from metal (normally bronze, brass, iron or other metal), that may or may not have a rim or turned over edge, that may or may not have a hammered out centre (boss, dome, nipple or cupola) and that may or may not be tuned to a specific note on a musical scale.

TAM-TAM

The accepted definition of a tam-tam is a 'flat-faced gong of indefinite pitch'. In other words, it does not have a boss/dome/nipple/cupola at its centre and may or may not have a turned over rim and has not been tuned to a specific pitch. Where a rim exists, it is only shallow in depth, normally no more than a few centimetres.

Examples of tam-tams with rims are the Paiste Symphonic Gong and the Chinese 'Chao' gong. Note that the 'Chinese' gongs marketed by Zildjian, Sabian and Stagg are in fact 'branded' Chao gongs from a number of gong makers located in the city of Wuhan in China. Examples of rimless tam-tams are those from VIBRA and UFIP in Italy and the 'Wind (Feng)' and 'Sun' gongs from Wuhan in China.

The characteristics of a tam-tam are a low fundamental note of indefinite pitch followed by a splash or crash of sound with many harmonics and overtones, the sound increasing in volume *after* the instrument has been struck. The sound is often described as waves crashing onto a rocky shore.

TUNED GONG

Tuned gongs are normally described as gongs that have been tuned to a specific pitch. They usually have a hammered or pressed out centre of varying depth, often referred to as a boss, dome, nipple or cupola. They also have a rim of varying depth, from the shallow rim as found on a tamtam, to very deep rims sometimes greater in depth than the diameter of the gong itself. Some of the gongs found in the Javanese and Balinese gamelan orchestras have this particular characteristic.

The characteristics of tuned gongs are a clear note with little or no shimmer, overtones or multitude of frequencies. The pitch may be tuned to either a Western scale (normally A = 442Hz) or an Eastern scale (e.g. a pentatonic scale). The tone can often be described as 'bell like' or akin to that heard on a metallophone or chime bar.

Examples of gongs tuned to the Western scale are the Tuned Gong range from Paiste (sadly no longer made at time of writing) and their range of 'Planet' gongs, plus certain models of the gongs made by UFIP in Italy. Examples of tuned gongs from South-East Asia and the Far East include Thai, Burmese, Javanese and Vietnamese bossed gongs, Chinese Bao gongs, gamelan gongs and Tibetan temple gongs.

Just to complicate matters there are examples of gongs that fall between these two categories. There are some eastern gongs that are difficult to categorise, especially those that have flat faces like a tamtam, a deep rim like a tuned gong, and a tone somewhere between the two. Examples can be found in British antique shops often having lived a life as hotel dinner gongs! The Paiste Tuned Gongs, once available as a four-and-a-half octave set, have a boss and a shallow turned over rim. When struck *pianissimo* to *forte* the tone is bell-like with a few overtones or harmonics. Above *forte* however, some of these instruments begin to shimmer and splash like a tam-tam! This is even more noticeable when the instrument is struck on the flat face and not the boss. Paiste also produced a set of tuned gongs without bosses. Likewise, the 'Planet Gong' range from the same manufacturer are essentially tam-tams with a very strong fundamental note tuned to a particular pitch. This has been based on the orbits of the planets (see Chapter 4) but, beyond *mezzo forte,*

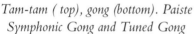

Tam-tam (top), gong (bottom). Paiste Symphonic Gong and Tuned Gong

Tam-tam (top), gong (bottom). Chinese Chao Gong, Thai Tuned Gong

sound just like their Symphonic Gong (tam-tam) counterparts! Chinese opera gongs have a shallow conical cross section with a flat top and when struck, the note rises or descends in pitch!

Confused? Well, as a way of illustrating the complexities, one can draw parallels with the Crocodilia family of reptiles. How many times have people in, for instance Europe, gone to the zoo and looked at an alligator and said "Look at that crocodile?" Likewise, how many people in the United States have gone to a zoo and said "Look at that 'gator", when they are actually looking at a caiman?

The Crocodilia family is split into four types – crocodiles, alligators, gavials and caiman. They are distinguished by the shape and size of the head and jaws as well as their distribution around the planet. Yet there are 25 sub-groups of these animals including Nile crocodiles, Salt Water crocodiles, American alligators and Chinese alligators to name a few. In a similar manner, we can split the gong family into tam-tams and tuned gongs with various types under each heading but a substantial number of instruments that straddle the two!

Throughout this book I will use the term gong when describing a general or generic concept and tuned gong or tam-tam when referring to orchestral or percussion concepts and ideas. When referring to gongs from particular manufacturers I will refer to them by their trade or catalogue name and attempt to qualify their grouping as tuned or tam-tam in brackets after the trade name e.g. Paiste Symphonic Gong (tam-tam). In this way, I hope to clarify the issue of gong or tam-tam.

3. HISTORY, EARLY USES AND MANUFACTURING OF THE GONG

3.1 HISTORY

Gongs are thought to have existed in various forms for several thousand years, being one of the earliest metal instruments known. Their origins probably stem from pools of molten copper, formed when copper ore in rocks being used as ovens melted and flowed onto the ground. The resulting 'disc' was struck and found to have certain crude sonorous properties. During the Bronze Age (roughly 4000–2000 BC) copper was alloyed with tin to give a tougher metal than pure copper. It was used for tools, weapons and shields (amongst other things) and a crude gong may have been discovered by beating a bronze shield as a form of communication or intimidation. Discs of bronze may have been used to represent the Sun in agricultural communities.

James Blades, the eminent British percussionist, in his excellent (and recently republished) book *Percussion Instruments and Their History*[1] suggests that the origin of the modern gong is a country known as 'Hsi Yu' located between Tibet and Burma, where it was mentioned in the 6th century during the reign of Emperor Hsuan Wu (AD 500–516). The Chinese were certainly capable of making high quality bronze drums by this time. There are claims that the gong arrived in China from the West, and in the book *Gong Yoga* by Mehtab Benton[2] suggests that a form of gong originated in Greece and moved east with Alexander the Great to India, thence to other parts of South-East Asia.

In Javanese mythology the gong was created by the god-king Sang Hyang Guru (AD230) who ruled Java from a palace on Mount Lawu. He needed to summon other gods and invented the gong to do so. For complex messages he created two other gongs thus forming the original gamelan[3]. By the 9th century, gong-making was well established in Java and other parts of the Malay Archipelago particularly around Semarang in Java. At least seven distinct shapes can be found in this part of the world. Other areas of gong manufacture established themselves in China, Burma and Annam (an area between south-east China and Vietnam).

I support the theory of the gong arriving in Indo-China from the West. The Bronze Age started in Mesopotamia around 4000BC. Copper was found in the Zagrus Mountains and tin was found in the Taurus Mountains in Anatolia (modern day Turkey). In fact the spiritual home of the cymbal, a close relative of the gong, is acknowledged to be Turkey. The Bronze Age did not start in China until 1600 BC and in Thailand and Vietnam about a hundred years later. Chinese Bronze Age workings were found along the Yellow and Yangtze rivers (the modern day centre of Chinese gong production, Wuhan, is located on the Yangtze River) and the Chinese soon became masters of producing high quality bronze drums as well as other bronze artefacts. By 500 BC examples could be found in south-east China and Vietnam. In his book *The Archaeology of Music in Ancient China*[4] covering a period from 1400 BC to AD 750, Fritz Kuttner makes no mention of gongs (apart from an episode described further in this chapter) but makes plenty of references to bronze bells, drums and cauldrons as well as jade Pi discs and various lithophones (stone percussion instruments). This gives weight to the theory that gong production didn't start in China until about the 6th century AD in the areas suggested by Blades and others.

I also have a lot of sympathy with Mehab Benton's theory of the gong originating in Greece. Alexander the Great reached the Indus Delta in c 327 BC. One of the main components of the Greek army was the hoplite soldier. The shield carried by hoplites was a large (~approximately 1m diameter) slightly convex wooden structure covered with a sheet of bronze, the shield being known as a 'hoplon'. This bronze sheet, when detached, has remarkable similarities to a tam-tam and the Greeks could have taken this form to use as an instrument. Shields captured during Alexander's campaigns may have been dismantled for the valuable metal and similarly treated. Perhaps these gongs were traded by civilisations in this region for the bronze drums produced in south-east China with the Chinese refining the design to the forms we know today.

3.2   EARLY USES

Gongs were used in a variety of ways by Eastern civilisations. They were used in dance, song and theatre, either as an accompaniment, sound effect or as a direction for the play. Gongs transmitted messages and signals, calling workers from the fields, signalling manoeuvres in an army formation, or calling out an alarm. Some references claim that some large gongs could be heard 50 miles (80 km) away! Gongs were also used to frighten away evil spirits and for healing purposes. The gongs produced today by Paiste are sometimes adorned with Chinese characters known as *Tai Loi* which roughly translate as 'Bringing in the Good, Banishing the Evil'. Touching a gong was thought to bring great fortune and strength and they were considered great talismans. These properties of healing and strength form the basis for the use of gongs by sound healers and therapists today. They were also used in funeral rites to clear the way to the afterlife and to stimulate the crown chakra, thereby allowing the soul to leave the body to the next level of existence. Gongs were also considered a statement of wealth, rank or property – the larger the gong the greater the status. In China and Japan they featured at the head of processions to announce the person approaching (the number of strokes on the gong and its size determined the status) as well as to clear people out of the way!

In the West, there was an awareness of gongs by the 16th century but their first recorded use was by the Frenchman François-Joseph Gossec in his 'Funeral Music for Mirabeau' in 1791. Cherubini used one in his Requiem in 1816, Rossini used one in Act 3 of *Armida* (1817) and by Bellini used one in his opera *Norma* (1831). A fantastic combination of cymbals and tam-tams was used by Berlioz in his Requiem (1837) in an almost atomic like explosion at the climax of the 'Tuba Mirum'. In fact, most Western classical music compositions use tam-tams rather than tuned gongs though Puccini scored for tuned gongs in *Turandot* and

Madame Butterfly. During the middle of the 20th century the use of tuned gongs became more widespread especially by composers such as Olivier Messiaen and Pierre Boulez.

3.3   EARLY MANUFACTURE

The art of making gongs was surrounded by great secrecy and mysticism. Making gongs required great skill and only certain families specialised in their manufacture, much like the making of samurai swords in Japan. The methods were handed down from father to son and many believed that the making of gongs required help from a 'higher source'. Hence, the process of manufacture became more ritualistic with meditation and offerings by the gong smith. Some considered that they were open to attack by malicious spirits and adopted other names during the forging process.

Most gongs of good quality were made from bronze using a formula of around 80% copper and 20% tin (sometimes known as 'bell metal'). Lesser gongs had smaller amounts of copper and extra amounts of tin, iron or lead. In Annam (in modern Vietnam), special gongs containing a good deal of silver were made. These had a far reaching sound and were light in colour. They were very expensive, about five times more expensive than a normal gong. In some parts of China, gold was added and these gongs were very valuable.

The main five processes in making a gong are pouring, hammering, smoothing, tuning and polishing/decorating. First, the constituent metals are heated together until molten and then poured into moulds or cast into a cake of metal. Then the metal is repeatedly heated and hammered – each hammering session lasting about 30 seconds with up to 150 sessions for a large gong – until the final shape is formed. Next the gong is quenched from a high temperature (the metal is cherry red in colour at this stage) by cold water. This renders the metal elastic but still strong, ready for the next process of hammering. Any major dents or peaks are filled with a resinous paste applied by red hot iron rods or smoothed by files and then the gong is allowed to rest for a period of time. It is then hammered by expert hammer strokes to produce the final tuning. The gong is then re-heated and allowed to cool slowly to give it a measure of hardness. Finally, the gong is polished and decorated. Favourite decorations are dragons – a four-toed dragon being acceptable for public use and a five-toed dragon being reserved for royal use.

The craftsmanship involved in making a gong cannot be underestimated and high quality instruments from a thousand years ago are highly sought after. One instrument has attained legendary status and is described by Fritz Kuttner in his book *The Archaeology of Music in Ancient China*[4]. In one of the appendices he recounts an occurrence at the Metropolitan Museum of Art in New York during the late 1940s. A seven-foot-diameter 'cymbal' (currently there is some debate that it was actually a form of wind gong) from the T'ang Dynasty (AD 618–906) was struck *pianissimo* on its edge. After some 60 seconds, the initial hum had reached a colossal triple *fortissimo* lasting some 10 to 15 seconds before decaying away to *forte*, followed by another *crescendo* to *fortissimo* some 90 seconds later before finally decaying rapidly away. The cymbal was on loan to the museum before the owner moved it to the instrument collection at Yale University at the end of the 1940s. During the early 1950s, the owner (or their representative) took it to California, ostensibly for use by a dance troupe. It has not been seen since despite extensive enquiries. Such astonishing acoustic properties almost defy the laws of physics and are an attribute to the phenomenal skill of its maker.

Modern methods of gongmaking will be discussed in the next few chapters, looking at the products of the Paiste factory in Germany, UFIP in Italy, the factories of the city of Wuhan in China, the smithies of Indonesia, gongs from other cymbal manufacturers and the creations of several individuals who are working with different metals and shapes.

REFERENCES – CHAPTER 3

1.   Blades, James *Percussion Instruments and Their History* The Bold Strummer, Ltd. 2005

2.   Benton, Mehta, *Gong Yoga – Healing and Enlightenment Through Sound* iUniverse, 2008.

3. Warsondiningrat, R.T. – Serat Weda Pradangga. Cited in Roth, A.R. 'New Compositions for Javanese Gamelan' University of Durham, Doctoral Thesis, 1986, page 4. (via Wikipedia.)

4. Kuttner, Fritz, *The Archaeology of Music in Ancient China – Two Thousand Years of Acoustical Experimentation, 1400 BC – AD 750* Paragon House, 1990.

4. MODERN GONG MAKERS AND THEIR INSTRUMENTS

This section covers some of the current and recent makers of gongs, their manufacturing techniques and the instruments produced. Whilst the list covered here is extensive, a book of this size cannot hope to cover every gong being made today. [Many instruments produced in South-East Asia are not included but please contact the author if gongs have been omitted, or with information about small foundries not covered here, so that future editions can be made more comprehensive.]

Before looking at individual manufacturers, it is worth providing some definitions to aid understanding of the manufacturing process described.

ALLOY

A mixture of primarily two or more metals (plus traces of non-metallic elements such as phosphorus or silicon), formed when the metals combine in a molten state. The metals do not chemically bond at the atomic or molecular level but connect at the crystalline lattice level, giving the appearance of a new metal. The form and structure of an alloy can have characteristics of the constituent metals (ductility, for instance) but can exhibit new properties e.g. strength. Common alloys are:-

Bronze: formed from copper and tin. The most common ratio is 80% copper, 20% tin, commercially known as 'B20' or bell metal. Other common formulas are B8 (92% copper, 8% tin) and B12 (88% copper, 12% tin). B20 is acoustically excellent for cymbals and gongs with a long sustain, clear tones, lots of shimmer, but it is very brittle and requires extensive working during the hammering and tempering stages to make the metal strong. B8 bronze is easier to work and is less brittle than B20, and a common misconception is that it is acoustically inferior. Both Paiste and Zildjian, however, have done extensive work with the formulation and processing of B8, and modern day B8 cymbals are approaching the quality of B20 cymbals from these manufacturers. B8 is not normally used in gong making, though UFIP have had some success with this alloy for their 'Art Gong' range and their current 'Tam-Tam Light' and 'Sheet Bronze Gong' range.

Brass: formed from copper and zinc. The amount of zinc varies quite markedly from 5 to 50%, the most common ratio being 37% zinc. There are many different types of 'brass'. Tonally inferior to bronze, it is sometimes used in budget cymbals and gongs, especially from the Far East. UFIP used brass for their larger size (32"/81cm and above) gongs in their Art Gong range and still use it for their larger sheet brass tam-tams and gongs which have surprising acoustic qualities.

Nickel Silver: formed from copper (60%), nickel (20%) and zinc (20%). This alloy (technically a 'brass') is also known as 'German Silver'. Paiste quote a formula in their catalogues and publicity material of 88% copper and 12% nickel known as 'NS12'. In metallurgical circles 'NS12' is not a recognised metallurgical coding, and in fact all Paiste gongs use a nickel silver formula of roughly 63% copper, 25% zinc and 12% nickel and have done for many decades.

ANNEALING

A method of toughening a metal by heating to remove internal stresses, crystalline defects and dislocations.

CASTING

Shaping of metal by pouring molten metal into a mould.

HOT FORGING

A technique for forcing two metals together at a red to white hot stage by repeated hammering and heating, though the metal never becomes molten. A common example of this method is the process used to make Samurai swords, where the metal is also folded to give a complex layered structure for great strength. Forging is also used to increase the strength of the metal by removing brittleness. This is achieved by hammering and forcing the crystalline structure closer together.

PLANNISHING

A hammering technique to smooth out dents in metals when the metal is cool. The hammers have a polished face so they don't scratch the metal.

QUENCHING

Rapid cooling of hot metal, usually in cold water. It can either render the metal elastic allowing it to be shaped by hammering without cracking in the case of copper based alloys or hardening the metal, in the case of steels. For B20 bronze, it must be quenched from a very narrow temperature window to produce the softening effect. Get it wrong and it becomes as brittle as glass.

ROLLING

A method of making ingots of metal into flatter sheets or plates. The metal is first heated before rolling, a process which can be repeated many times, dependant on the alloy. It has the effect of forcing the metal crystal structure closer together as well as aligning the crystals if the rolling direction is controlled.

4.1   PAISTE

4.1.1 Background

One company, more than any other, is associated with the production of some of the world's finest gongs – the firm of Paiste. Paiste (pronounced

Pie-stee) have been making gongs since the 1940s at their factory in Schacht-Audorf in north Germany. They are extensively used in British and European orchestras as well as by rock groups. They are particularly favoured by sound therapists due to the high quality workmanship and the purity of the metals used in their alloys. Paiste have extensive knowledge of the properties of alloys and production techniques for making the sheets of metal from which the gongs are made. Much of this knowledge has been acquired from times where good quality raw materials were in short supply, especially during the formative years of the company.

Estonian-born Michael Toomas Paiste established a music shop in St Petersburg in Russia around 1910. In addition to selling sheet music, records and instruments, some musical instrument repairs were undertaken. By 1917, Michael had returned to Tallinn, the capital of Estonia. His son, called Michael M Paiste, eventually joined the firm in 1927 and took over in 1928. Paiste had started to produce cymbals in the Turkish style by this time and as well as the first gongs. The first exports to Europe and the USA taking place in 1932. The family of Michael M moved to Poland in 1939, fearing an invasion of Estonia by Russia (which eventually happened) only for Poland to be invaded by Germany in the same year. Most of their cymbal production in the war years went to Germany though some exports were made. At the end of the war, the family were considering a move to either Canada or Sweden but established the factory in northern Germany following funding via the Marshall Plan. Cymbal production started again in 1947 and a new cymbal production facility (and company headquarters) was established in Switzerland (Nottwil) in 1957 with Michael M's sons, Robert and Toomas. The current directors are Robert Paiste and Toomas' Son, Erik Paiste.

Early gong production started with nickel silver but it was rumoured that by the 1960s this had changed to bronze using a ratio of 68% copper, 24% tin and 8% nickel. This rumour formed partly due to this formula being reported in James Blades percussion book (see reference 1 in Chapter 3). In fact, nickel silver to a formula of 63% copper, 25% zinc and 12% nickel (give or take the odd percentage or part percentage) has been used throughout the company's history. This is based on analysis of metal taken from three Symphonic Gongs made in the 1960s, 1990s and 2010 that I had carried out in order to lay to rest once and for all the speculation about Paiste gong metal that can be found on various websites. Even Paiste quotes 'NS12' in their literature with a formula of 88% copper and 12% nickel, but NS12 is not a recognised coding in metallurgy circles and 88% copper and 12% nickel is in fact a cupro-nickel, not nickel silver which is a copper/zinc/nickel-based metal.

Collectors of gongs often remark on the tonal differences between 'old' and 'new' Paiste gongs and often attribute this to an aging process, which may be true in part, but is more likely to be due to the crystalline structure and minor differences in the basic elements used. Also, the rolling processes have been improved over time allowing Paiste to move to a slightly thinner gauge metal without loss of strength in the gong. The use of nickel in the formula is particularly pleasing to sound therapists as in ancient times, nickel was considered a 'metal from the Universe' due to it being found in large amounts in meteorites. It is also considered to bring a bright and pure tone to these instruments compared with other gongs that do not contain nickel.

Important factors involved in the production of good quality alloys are grain size, grain structure, grain alignment and alloy hardness, which are determined by the casting, rolling and annealing processes. One technique developed by Paiste is a method of rolling to align the grain structure, which results in a longer 'speaking time' and decay of the sound compared to an equivalent Chinese 'Chao' gong. Even to a partially trained ear, it is possible to differentiate between a Paiste tam-tam and a Wuhan tam-tam on a recording.

Some of the alloys used by Paiste, such as the 'Sound Formula' and 'Signature Bronze' alloy used in cymbals, are patented. In fact, a lot of formulae quoted on websites devoted to gongs often quote formulae used by Paiste for their cymbal ranges, most of which are bronze and quite extensive, and put Paiste amongst the top three cymbal manufactures in terms of production in the world.

During the 1950s and 1960s, Paiste had a team of gong makers but it wasn't until the 1970s that the concept of a 'master' gong maker came into being. This is essentially one of the team being responsible for fine tuning the gongs, developing concepts or interpreting customer's requests. At certain times this has meant more than one 'master gong maker' being present at the factory in addition to any input from Robert and Toomas! Rudi Bonness was one of the first master gong makers and others have included Heiko Palkus, Heinz Jessat, Walter Meyer and Broder Oetken. The current gong master is Sven Meier. It is fair to say that these gentlemen live and breathe gongs and have had a profound influence on the development of gongs in the West in the last four decades. Even when the gong maker has retired, they often call into the factory to give the team the benefit of their experience.

Paiste currently has three teams of two men making gongs at present. A two-man team is sufficient for gongs up to 40"/102cm in diameter but all six could be used to make a 60"/152cm or 80"/203cm gong. They are currently at maximum capacity making gongs, working one hour per day extra plus a half day on Saturdays, such is the demand for Paiste gongs. Gong production is around 120 per month, or about five per working day.

4.1.2 Manufacture

First the selected alloy is cast into a round ingot before being heated and rolled in a rolling mill to form sheets of metal. This heating and rolling of the metal forces the crystalline structure together and aligns its structure thereby enhancing the sound properties of the gong as well as strengthening its physical capabilities. This allows the sheets to be turned into gongs without fracturing or cracking during the hammering process. Paiste works with several foundries to produce the metal it requires to ensure consistent quality and availability.

The gongs start off as circular discs or 'blanks' cut from the metal sheets. The gauge or thickness of the metal determines the size of the gong – larger gongs need thicker metal. Following degreasing and cleaning, the blanks are then marked with three concentric circles using a scribing tool. The position of these marks is determined by a bespoke stiff leather template for each gong size. The first circle is near the edge of the gong and marks where the rim will be formed. The next one is a few centimetres inwards of the rim mark, and marks the position of where the 'face' of the gong will be formed as well as the starting point for the tuning of the gong. The third mark is near the centre and marks the point where the centre disc starts and the tuning marks will end. The centre and edges of the sheets are then heated to a high temperature using a gas torch – the centre to a 'warm' red, the edge to a higher temperature. This allows the edges to be formed without splitting, and the centre to flex with the tension that will

Nickel Silver blanks at the Paiste factory

be put into the gong during the hammering process. It also helps the boss of a tuned gong to be formed. In addition, the colour of the flame also gives rise to the characteristic brown colour to the edges and centre of Paiste gongs.

Heat treated nickel silver blanks

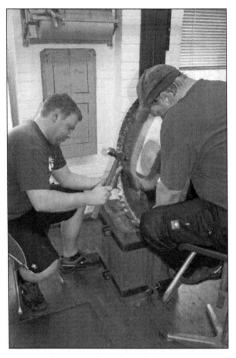

Forming the edge of the gong

The edge is first formed by hammering along the outer circular mark around the gong using metal wedge shaped hammers. A large block of wood with a groove cut into it (essentially a wooden anvil) helps turn the edge over. Two people are needed for this process – one hammering, and one holding and moving the gong round. The hammering technique 'pulls' the metal over the rim almost like the tightening of a skin on a drum, so the rim becomes the frame of the gong and the face is then allowed to 'vibrate'. This process tensions the gong out towards the rim and the amount of tensioning varies between gong types, the Symphonic Gongs being more tensioned than the Planet Gongs. You can see these marks on the rear of the gong (where all the hammering is done) as the elliptical-shaped marks at the rim. The face of the gong from the rim to the second circular marking is then hammered with a large hammer with a large flat face, which has the effect of sending the tension towards the centre of the gong. The rough hammer marks (along the edge and the inner flat face adjacent to the edge) are then smoothed out using a ball pein hammer against a wooden block.

Once the edge has been formed, the gong is placed face down on another block of wood covered with cloth. The rear face is hammered from the second circular mark by a series of blows, one man hammering and another turning the gong. A second set of hammering follows inwards of the first set, slightly further apart and lighter in force, followed by a third set even more spaced apart and lighter in force again, followed by a final fourth set just outside the third inner circular mark. This process has the effect of forming the slightly stepped out face of the gong, evening up the tension in the metal and adding a modicum of tuning to the gong. Between each set of hammering, the face of the gong is checked for squareness. For the Planet Gongs, the tuning is checked by a microphone and electronic tuning device, the tunings having been worked out from Hans Cousto's calculations (see section on Planet Gongs) plus corrections made for the size of the gong and the note's percentage deviation from the

Checking the tuning of the gong

Tuning the gong. Note the circles as visual aids for the three concentric tuning bands.

note 'A' tuned to 442 Hz. The tuning is adjusted by further hammering along the second circular mark with a different weighting to each blow, each subsequent hammering raising the pitch of the note. Fine tuning is done with light blows.

Once rested (normally a day), the gong is decorated by a smith who scrapes the vertical pattern found on the front face, using a sharp tool. Fine tuning of the gong is carried out by careful hammering before screen printing of any markings (Paiste logo, Tai Loi characters or astrological symbols). A final clean and polish using Bohrer Wax takes place before the product is shipped to the distributers for final delivery to customers.

Marking the face of the gong

Making the gongs is quite hazardous. Ear plugs or ear defenders must be worn in the vicinity of the hammering, which is very loud. Repetitive strain injury and vibration injury from the hammering process are common medical problems.

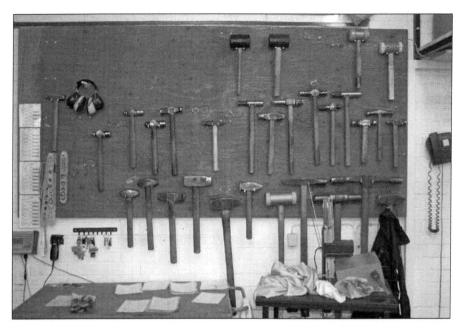

The gong maker's tools – lots of hammers!

The author with the Paiste gong making team, September 2011
(Photo courtesy of Pauline McCrann)

4.1.3   Symphonic Gongs (tam-tams)

The Symphonic Gongs are probably the most recognisable of the Paiste range and certainly the most widespread, though the Planet Gong range is becoming much more common. Symphonic Gongs are used by practically every professional orchestra in the UK as well as many brass bands, wind bands and amateur orchestras. They are also used widely in many Western European orchestras but not by all. Some of the big name orchestras in Europe including the Berlin Philharmonic, Vienna Philharmonic and Amsterdam Concertgebouw orchestras use Chao gongs (tam-tams). In the United States, most orchestras use Chao gongs from Zildjian, Sabian or directly imported from China. Many American percussionists and conductors prefer the sound of a Chao gong. Indeed, when Gerald Schwarz took over as conductor of the Royal Liverpool Philharmonic Orchestra, the percussion section had to acquire three Chao tam-tams and recordings of pieces performed by this orchestra during this period use these instruments.

Many rock groups use Paiste Symphonic Gongs, one of the more famous being the one used by Roger Taylor at the end of Queen's 'Bohemian Rhapsody'.

The Symphonic Gong is flat faced and unpitched (though Paiste say there is an element of pitch) and is similar to the Chinese Chao gong. It has a wide frequency range with washing highs, swelling overtones and harmonics, and a long sustain. The *pianissimo* note on a large Symphonic Gong is a lovely 'boom' sound. A *forte* note has a crashing, swelling high, the maximum volume being reached *after* the note has been struck. The response is fast but not as fast as an equivalent Chao gong. Physically, the gong has a slightly raised but flat face with a shallow but heavily hammered rim. The centre of the gong is brown in colour and undecorated, the rim being a similar colour. The section between the centre and rim is a whitish gold colour with vertical striping made with a sharp tool, and it is highly polished. The face of the gong can be marked with the Paiste logo or the Chinese 'Tai Loi' characters which tend to be favoured by sound healers. Symphonic Gongs are a good starting point for a gong collection as their range of sounds encompasses many aspects of the gong.

Symphonic gongs are available in the following sizes: 20"/51cm, 22"/56cm, 24"/61cm, 26"/66cm, 28"/71cm, 30"/76cm, 32"/81cm, 34"/86cm, 36"/91cm, 38"/96cm, 40"/102cm, 50"/127cm, 60"/152cm and 80"/203cm. The 80" Symphonic Gong is the world's largest commercially available gong. The 60" Symphonic Gong is available in two versions – a standard symphonic and a thinner rimmed version called 'SGM'. The 'M' stands for 'Mikrophonie' and is a reference to the composer Karlheinz Stockhausen and his celebrated 1960 composition *Mikrophonie I*. This gong was specially commissioned for the piece and was made in collaboration between Robert Paiste and Stockhausen. It has a slightly faster response than the standard 60" but still retains the depth of sound found on these large gongs. The standard 60" Symphonic Gong has an 8cm-deep rim, the SGM has a 4cm-deep rim.

The smaller gongs (20"/51cm – 24"/61cm) have a strong fundamental note and the *fortissimo* crash is short-lived. They are mainly used as 'colour' in classical music compositions but are too small to use as the main tam-tam in the classical music repertoire. Equally, their limited frequency range has some drawbacks when used for sound healing though several practitioners and yoga class instructors regularly use 24" Symphonic Gongs. Their small size and weight, however, makes them ideal for use as 'walking' gongs in sound healing practices (see Chapter 8).

The mid-size gongs (26"/66cm – 32"/ 81cm) have a pleasant balance of fundamental note and crashing highs. This range is a bit small for use as the standard orchestral tam-tam, as the *pianissimo* note will not penetrate the orchestra sufficiently and the *fortissimo* crash 'speaks' too quickly. That said, I used a 32" model for a number of years in a couple of amateur orchestras without too many problems. They are, however, very useful as the smaller of the two tam-tams required in Mahler's Symphony No.2 and the middle of the three tam-tams needed for a number of pieces written by Olivier Messiaen. A 32" Symphonic is often a better choice, in my opinion, for the tam-tam part in Stravinsky's *The Rite of Spring* as it is far easier to control, especially in the 'Procession of the Sage' and 'Sacrificial Dance' sections. The 26" – 32" range is often a better choice for use in a theatre pit orchestra and for brass and wind bands. Anything bigger than a 32" gong becomes harder to transport, especially for band contests where a band may only have two minutes to set up before playing.

Portability is the key word for this size of gong which is especially useful for sound therapists. They can be taken to venues both indoor and outdoor and are useful in modern houses with their smaller rooms. They also have a good frequency range for use as healing instruments. As a guide:-

Theatre Pit Work:	28", 30" (71cm, 76cm)
Brass Band/Wind Band:	30", 32" (76cm, 81cm)
Sound Therapy:	28" – 32" (71cm, 81cm)
Second Orchestral tam-tam:	30", 32" (76cm, 81cm)

If you could afford just one Symphonic Gong, my recommendation is to go for a 32"/81cm model.

The larger size gongs (34"/86cm to 40"/102cm) are the sizes that find most use within symphony orchestras, especially the 36" and 38" models. Beyond these sizes, the price rises significantly. A 36" or 38" model will cover most of the classical repertoire more than adequately. Sound therapists are also using the 36" and 38" models to form the core of their collection. The range of tones, harmonics and frequencies encompasses all aspects of 'human energy interactions' as well as emitting a physical sound pressure wave that is beneficial in healing. Their drawbacks, if any, are their size and weight, which make them difficult to transport and set up. They need to be well supported on a good quality, strong stand.

The top end of the range – 50"/127cm, 60"/152cm, 60"SGM and the colossal 80"/203cm Symphonic Gong should be seen as specialised instruments. They have a formidable physical presence both visually and acoustically. They are also rarely seen! They are too big for most musical applications as they take a very long time to 'speak' and take up a lot of room. Curiously, although one would initially have thought about using one of these instruments for the loud crashes at the end of the second

An array of Paiste Symphonic Gongs

movement of Respighi's *Church Windows* or the eighth movement of Messiaen's *Turangalila Symphony*, they have, in reality, only occasionally been used in concerts and then only for very quiet notes. Their size means that the *pianissimo* note can penetrate an orchestra very effectively. Stockhausen specified a 60" Symphonic Gong from Paiste for his work *Mikrophonie I*. The work is scored for one large tam-tam, two players, two microphones and a mixing desk, amplifier and speakers.

The commonest use for these larger instruments is in the field of sound healing. The instruments possess complex sounds, tones, harmonics and frequencies and a 'presence' that demands respect. I had always dreamt that the first time I played one of these instruments, I would indulge myself with a hefty thwack with a No. 8 Paiste gong mallet. In reality, I was so overawed by the sheer presence of a 60" Symphonic Gong that I confined myself to soft beats with a No.6 mallet and never got it above *mezzo piano*. Drawing a small 'flumi' across its face gave an eerie, whale song sound that disappeared into an infinity that seemed to exist beyond the back face of the gong.

The 80" Symphonic is the world's largest production gong and is a very rare beast. Current estimates say that four exist in the UK. One belongs to Bell Percussion in London and is available for hire, if you have the room! Another belongs to a sound healer in London and is known as the 'golden gong' because of its surface finish.

(l-r) Paiste 50", 60" Mikrophonie and 80" Symphonic Gongs

The latest development with the Symphonic Gong is the 'SG Brilliant'. These gongs have been polished with a buffing tool to produce a bright mirror finish on the gongs. The buffing process removes some of the metal and adds a bit of heat into the metal, so the tone is slightly brighter (musically) than a standard Symphonic Gong. They may require more looking after, in terms of cleaning and removing finger marks etc. During my visit to the Paiste factory, they had a 32" SG Brilliant hanging outside in the garden to look at the longer term effects of the weather on the finish of these gongs. I think it is fair to say that these gongs are aimed more at sound healers and other esoteric uses than the symphony orchestra or rock group, but they nevertheless have a certain physical presence that would enhance any surrounding that they could be used in.

Paiste Symphonic Gong 'Brilliant'

4.1.4 Planet Gongs (tam–tams)

In the 1980s, Paiste started to develop a range of gongs aimed at sound healing and meditation practitioners. In appearance they look just like Symphonic Gongs, but when they are played they have a much stronger fundamental tone. This fundamental tone is tuned to a specific pitch based on a natural harmonic series derived from the orbital properties of the Sun, Moon, Earth and other planets and planetoids in our Solar System. These frequencies were calculated by the Swiss mathematician Hans Cousto and explained in his book *The Cosmic Octave – the Origin of Harmony*[1], though the frequencies for 'Chiron', 'Sedna' and 'Niburu' are thought to have been the work of the Kairos Institute of Sound Healing in New Mexico, USA. The range was suggested by Jens Zygar, a colleague of Johannes Heimrath and schoolmate of Erik Paiste following the publication of the Cousto book. Cousto had already developed a set of tuning forks matched to his planetary frequencies and Zygar considered that a set of gongs tuned to the same frequencies would complement the tuning forks. The gongs were available by 1992.

The gongs themselves are actually tuned an octave below Cousto's frequencies and Table 1 shows the nearest tuning based on the Western scale (A4=440/442 Hz) that most of us are familiar with. In reality, the tuning is not that stable and is rapidly lost, especially by overplaying.

According to Paiste, the Planet Gongs resonate with the cycles of the cosmos – the so-called 'music of the spheres'. They are made from the same nickel silver alloy as the Symphonic Gongs, but with a slightly different hammering/tuning process. They are decorated in the centre with the astrological symbol for the particular planet or celestial body and normally don't carry the Paiste logo. Since their introduction, the diameters of some of the planet gongs have been reduced, possibly to make the range a bit more affordable to customers. The range has also been added to since their inception. 'Sedna' and 'Chiron' are large asteroids/planetoids which are now known to have astrological influences, and 'Niburu' is the 'missing planet' or 'Planet X' which is thought to have a 3,000-year orbit and causes major physical effects on the Earth when it returns. They are certainly a growth area for Paiste and, at the time of writing, a three month wait for a Planet Gong was not unexpected.

TABLE 1 – PAISTE PLANET GONGS

Planet Gong	Present Diameter (inches)	Previous Diameter (inches)	Cousto Frequency Hz	Pitch of actual gong (A4=442 Hz)
Sun	38"	-	126.22	B1
Sedna	38"	-	128.10	C2
Earth	38"	-	136.10	C# 2
Pluto	36"	-	140.25	C# 2
Mercury	32"	34"	141.27	C# 2
Mars	32"	34"	144.72	D2
Saturn	32"	34"	147.85	D2
Chiron	32"	-	151.27	D# 2
Niburu	32"	-	161.26	E2
Platonic Year	30"	32"	172.06	F2

TABLE 1 – PAISTE PLANET GONGS – Continued

Planet Gong	Present Diameter (inches)	Previous Diameter (inches)	Cousto Frequency Hz	Pitch of actual gong (A4=442 Hz)
Jupiter	28"	30"	183.58	F# 2
Sidereal Earth Day	28"	-	194.71	G2
Uranus	24"	26"	207.36	G# 2
Synodic Moon	24"	26"	210.42	G# 2
Neptune	24"	26"	211.44	G# 2
Venus	24"	26"	221.23	A
Sidereal Moon	24"	-	227.43	A# 2

Note that the actual pitch of the gong is an octave BELOW that specified by Cousto and Kairos.

Sound healers, yoga, meditation and alternative therapy practitioners use these gongs in a variety of ways and often describe physical effects and characteristics associated with a particular gong. There are various books such as *Gongs of our Solar System*[2] by gongmaster Don Conreaux, and various websites of sound healers and other individuals involved in this fascinating area. Table 2 contains a detailed selection of the more commonly occurring characteristics. Astrological signs in brackets indicate the originally assigned sign from when astrology only dealt with the visible planets as far as Saturn.

TABLE 2 – PLANET GONG CHARACTERISTICS

Planet Gong	Astrological Sign	Characteristics
Sun	Leo	Self, vitality, core essence, cutting negativity, purifying
Sedna	-	
Earth	-	Compassion, love, acceptance, fulfilment
Pluto	Scorpio	Transformation, growth, transcendence
Mars	Aries (Scorpio)	Action, energy, accomplishment
Saturn	Capricorn, (Aquarius)	Stability, patience, structure, discipline

TABLE 2 – PLANET GONG CHARACTERISTICS – Continued

Planet Gong	Astrological Sign	Characteristics
Mercury	Gemini, Virgo	Mind, knowledge, understanding, communication
Niburu	–	Change on a grand scale
Chiron	–	Overcoming, heroic behaviour, maverick, healing
Platonic Year	–	365 day gong, cosmic consciousness, enlightenment
Jupiter	Sagittarius (Pisces)	Expansion, evolution, journey
Day – Sidereal	–	Security, stability
Uranus	Aquarius	Change, innovation, awakening, raising awareness
Neptune	Pisces	Mystic, dreams, psychic, spiritual awareness
Moon Synodic (New Moon)	Cancer	Feelings, emotional balance, feminine needs
Venus	Taurus Libra	Relationships, attraction, harmony, gentleness, love
Moon – Sidereal (Full Moon)	Cancer	Feelings, fullness, completeness, feminine emotions

An array of Paiste Planet Gongs. Top (l-r) Sedna, Pluto, Saturn, Mars, Earth. Bottom (l-r) Uranus, Chiron, Platonic Year and New Moon

4.1.5 Sound Creation Gongs

The genesis of the Sound Creation Gongs can be traced back to the late 1960s when, so the story goes, sales of the Symphonic Gong had reached a steady, if somewhat low level. Robert and Toomas started to experiment freely and the other gong makers at Paiste tried various shapes and hammering methods to try and create new and exciting sounds. The Swiss musician Henriette Cron worked with Robert Paiste at the Nottwil, Switzerland workshops to refine the sounds of the gongs, and the percussionist Michael Jüllich gave a lot of input from his experience of playing Paiste gongs. In 1978, Johannes Heimrath, author the excellent book *The Healing Power of the Gong*[3], (a recommended text for sound healers everywhere), began working with Paiste, further developing the sound and appearances of the gongs.

Initially, a set of ten 'proto' or prototype gongs were created as a result of these various experiments. These prototypes were then presented to various audiences in seminars, music schools etc who then filled in questionnaires asking them to describe a representation of the sound. The gongs were then marketed according to the groupings of these sounds and other esoteric feelings, using descriptions like 'Sun', 'Moon', 'Fire' etc. The words used by Paiste to describe the gongs in their catalogues are 'unimaginable, esoteric and mysterious'.

The original range consisted of ten gongs (plus four versions of the No. 3 'Earth' gong). Some were originally made in a smaller diameter but visually similar to other gongs in the range. For instance, the early 'Confrontation' gong looked visually similar to the 'Moon' gong but it was smaller and made from thinner metal. The Moon Gong eventually received an enhanced shape which produced more overtones, and the Confrontation Gong received a hammered ring, giving it a richer, angrier sound and helped distinguish it from the small Earth Gong.

At the present time, only the four 'Earth' gongs plus the Nos. 8, 9 and 10 'Chakra' gongs are available. The full range was certainly available in 1996 but in the Year 2000 catalogue, the No. 1 and No. 6 gongs were missing, and the Nos. 2, 5 and 7 gongs were only available by special order. The reason for this was that many of the gongs were the speciality

A set of 'master' Sound Creation Gongs at the Paiste factory.
Top (l-r) Sun, Moon, Earth (26"), Water
Bottom (l-r) Peace, Fire, Confrontation and the three Chakra gongs

A 60" Earth Sound Creation Gong

of certain master gong makers at Paiste. The Fire and Moon Gongs (SCG Nos. 2 and 6) were the speciality of Heiko Palkus so when he left, these were the first gongs to disappear from the catalogue. The Sun, Peace and Confrontation Gongs (SCG Nos. 1,5 and 7) were the speciality of Walter Meyer who left a couple of years after Heiko, and these too eventually disappeared from the catalogues.

The Sound Creation Gongs occasionally appear on web-based auction sites, often selling for substantial sums of money, partly due to their rarity and partly (in my opinion) due to them being the favoured gongs of Johannes Heimrath. Inspired by Johannes work, many sound healers have attached certain characteristics, effects and attributes to these gongs (as in the original consultation when they were being developed) and some of the more common attributes are noted in the following descriptions.

SCG No. 1 'Sun'

Diameter 22"/56cm. It is tuned to a strong fundamental of C sharp. It has an unusual double-stepped rim and the surface has scraped markings and is heavily hammered. It has a nice, warm, sustained fundamental with a bright, almost howling *fortissimo* plus a radiating bell-like tone. It has a long decay for such a small instrument, but there is little splash or crashy overtones with this gong.

Related attributes – energy giving, stimulating, motivating.

SCG No.2 'Fire'

Diameter 20" /51cm. The fundamental note is not tuned to any particular pitch. It has a single stepped rim and three hammered out 'spokes' radiating from the centre. The scraped markings also radiate out from the centre. This gong has a warm fundamental with roaring highs. Many overtones are produced, especially when using harder mallets.

Related attributes – warm, protecting, centred (when played quietly), aggressive, destructive, cutting (when played loudly).

SCG No.3 'Earth'

Available in four sizes – No.3 (26"/66cm), No.3A (32"/81cm), No.3B (38"/96cm) and No.3C (60"/152cm). The appearance of these gongs is very dark, both in terms of colour and sound. The surface is full of prominent hammer marks and there are no scraped areas. They have very warm, dark fundamentals, roaring highs and a long, dry sustain, though not as long as that found in an equivalent Symphonic Gong. They are very similar in sound to the Chinese Chao gongs, but without the metallic jangling, and have a much longer decay. Size for size, the metal is thicker than their equivalent Symphonic Gong counterpart so you essentially get a much deeper gong sound for a particular size. For instance, a 38" SCG Earth has a deep fundamental note on a par with a 40" Symphonic. They are also considerably more expensive than a Symphonic equivalent. For those few lucky enough to have heard the rare 60" version, this is considered to be the best gong made by Paiste, though that is a matter of personal taste.

Related attributes – opening the heart centre, remembering who we are, continuity, connectivity.

SCG No.4 'Water'

This gong has a diameter of 24"/61cm. It is not tuned but has a reverse boss and a radially scraped surface. The fundamental is a soft round sound until *mezzo-forte* is reached. After this the crash becomes they key sound, with plenty of wash, flowing frothy sound with a slow decay. The rock group Toto used this gong in their hit single 'Africa'.

Related attributes – moving stagnant energies, clearing, cleansing.

SCG No.5 'Peace'

Gong diameter 22"/56cm. Originally made as a 20"/51cm diameter gong, it has the same colourings as a Symphonic Gong but has a much closer scraped and hammered face. This face protrudes more than a Symphonic Gong. It has soft lows with various layers building up to harmonious highs, but never aggressive. It sounds very much like an equivalent size Chao gong.

Related attributes – calming, restful, peace.

SCG No.6 'Moon'

Gong diameter 24"/61cm. It is a flat gong with a heavily scraped and hammered face and a deeper rim compared to an equivalent Symphonic Gong. The metal is also slightly thicker. The fundamental is tuned to F sharp and is very strong. It has a full, dense balanced sound, ringing highs, a dark bell-like tone and a long, long decay. There is no crash or splash.

Related attributes – enveloping, shielding, protection, support (especially hormonal systems).

SCG No.7 'Fight/Confrontation'

Gong diameter 22"/51cm. A flat gong with a scraped wavy surface and distinct hammer marks both on the rear and the front surface. There is a raised ring between edge and face of the gong. It has crashing, raw highs which decay in a threatening way. Needs to be controlled as it 'speaks' very easily. Curiously, 'Confrontation' was originally produced as a 20"/51cm diameter gong with a physical appearance of SCG No.6 'Moon' but with a smaller depth rim.

Related attributes – bringing issues to the fore, confronting problems, releasing suppressed emotions.

The original design for SCG No. 7 (top) and the later design (bottom)

SCG Nos. 8, 9 and 10. 'Chakra'

Head/Forehead – 11"/28cm diameter

Chest/Larynx – 14"/36cm diameter

Abdomen/Breastbone – 16"/40cm diameter

Heavy gongs with boss and a bright finish. They have a distinct fundamental tone, harmonics, ringing penetrating sound and are distinctly bell-like. Reminiscent of Balinese and other South East Asian tuned gongs but lighter in weight than their equivalent Asian brothers. Ideally suited to those healers working with the Chakras.

4.1.6 Tuned Gongs

Paiste also used to produce a ranged of tuned or bossed gongs. The range was spread over four-and-a-half octaves ranging from C2 to F6 and diameters from 36"/91cm down to 6"/15cm. Apart from the boss, the gongs looked similar to the Symphonic Gongs with scraped faces, hammered edges and turned over rims and the same brown/gold colourations. The tuning was to either 440 or 442Hz A. Each gong had a specific fundamental note, very bell-like but had a tendency to 'splash' when played above *forte*. Paiste called this 'cushioning softly by complimentary gong harmonics'. Hence, when they were played loudly, they tended to sound more like tam-tams than tuned gongs. I found this sound confusing during my early years of gong research, when I was trying to determine the difference between a gong and a tam-tam by just *listening* to performances using these gongs. It wasn't until I saw the Halle Orchestra playing Michael Tippett's Triple Concerto that I was able to examine this type of gong at close hand. It is possible that some of these gongs that I heard on recordings were suffering from 'metal fatigue' (see Chapter 7) as a result of overplaying, as I have recently purchased some direct from the Paiste factory that had been 'forgotten' in a stock room and they don't have the splashy overtones.

It is thought that the production of tuned gongs came about after a member of the Paiste factory visited Java in 1959 at the behest of the Indonesian Embassy in Germany who were looking to acquire a gamelan (an Indonesian orchestra which numbers many gongs amongst its instruments –see Chapter 5). By 1963 Paiste were producing their own tuned gongs, but it was Walter Meyer that developed the tuned gong range into what we know today. He was responding to requests from composers and percussionists who required a tuned gong that had a lot more sustain and volume than the South-East Asian tuned gongs. Walter found that the height of the boss was not the determining factor in its tuning – it was the width of the boss coupled with the width of the surrounding metal between the boss and the rim. A wide boss and narrow metal surround gives a higher pitch, and a narrower boss plus a wider metal surround results in a lower pitch.

The gongs are no longer made, though they occasionally turn up on web-based auction sites at somewhat inflated prices, though they were very expensive when new, especially the smaller diameters. Those that do exist in quantity tend to belong to percussion hire shops. Bell Percussion in London has the full range available for hire at reasonable prices.

There is a limited calling for these gongs in orchestral music, mainly being restricted to 20th century works and avant-garde music, particularly of the 1950s to 1980s. They are used extensively in

A pair of Paiste Tuned Gongs

works by Olivier Messiaen. Four are used in 'Des Canyons aux Etoiles', six in *Et Exspecto* and seven are used (plus three tam-tams) to dramatic effect in *Resurrection of Our Lord Jesus Christ*. In latter years, the increased availability of cast gongs from Thailand, Burma and Vietnam with their associated lower costs have somewhat taken over from the Paiste tuned gong for those who need such instruments. Also, the Planet Gong range with their strong fundamental notes tuned to a one octave scale from B1–A#2 has also spelled the demise of these gongs. Having heard recordings of Messiaen's works played with both Paiste and Burmese gongs, I have a preference for the Paiste tuned gong with its unique sound crossover of tuned gong and tam-tam. Burmese gongs should never be played loud and produce a 'clang' like sound when they are.

For a short period during late 1970s to 1980s, Paiste also produced a set of flat faced tuned gongs(!) to be played horizontally like a Burmese Gong Play. They were available in either a one octave set (C4-C5) or a one-and-a-half octave set (C4-F5).

4.1.7 Accent and Deco Gongs

Completing the Paiste range are a small number of gongs designed for percussive 'effects' and decoration. The 'Accent' gongs are like Symphonic Gongs but are made from thinner gauge metal with a focussed sound and rapid crash. They are available in 7"/18cm, 10"/25cm, 13"/33cm and 22"/56cm sizes.

The 'Deco' gongs are similar to accent gongs but are more for decoration, coming with a small version of the Paiste 'floor' stand. According to the Paiste catalogues, they are made in the same manner as the symphonic gongs. They are available in 7"/18cm, 10"/25cm and 13"/33cm diameters and formerly a 16"/41cm size.

4.2 UFIP

4.2.1 Background

Somewhat overshadowed by their European counterparts at Paiste, UFIP are nevertheless part of the European gong-making tradition. Bronze working in the area around Pistoia in Italy can be traced back nearly 4,000 years to the Etruscans. Centuries later, during the 1700s, the Tronci family were using bronze in pipe organs. They had a long tradition of bell making dating back to the Renaissance and, by the 1800s, they had expanded into chimes, bells and cymbals with the demise of large pipe organs. The great Italian opera composers such as Puccini, Verdi and Mascagni commissioned large gongs and tam-tams for their operas (e.g. Puccini uses large tuned gongs in *Turandot*).

There were other family-based manufacturers of bronze instruments in Pistoia and Florentino. In 1927 the families started to work together to bring modern technologies into metal-working processes, and in 1931 they formed a co-operative to set standards that would generate them a future and end commercial rivalry. The four founding companies were Marredi Benti, Zanchi & Biesai, Rosati Leopoldo and A&B Tronci Brothers. The co-operative adopted the name of UFIP – Unione Fabricanti Italiani di Piatti musicali e tam-tams.

During the Second World War, imports of copper and tin became scarce. The Italian government upheld orders of cymbals for military bands but UFIP had to experiment with other metals such as iron. The poor tonal qualities of such instruments however, resulted in the government giving UFIP an authorisation to obtain supplies of copper and tin. In 1968, the co-operative became UFIP Ltd.

Like Paiste, experimentation and technological advances in casting are a hallmark of UFIP. Their biggest technological step forward was the introduction of the Rotocasting system developed by Mariano and Lindano Zanchi. Unlike traditional casting where the molten bronze is poured into a static mould, in rotocasting, the mould is rotated at high speeds (up to 1000 rpm). As the liquid is poured into the moulds, the impurities are 'spun' to the outer edges of the cymbal by centrifugal forces. These impurities are removed by lathing (known as 'peeling') and the resulting metal disc has a much more compact crystalline structure compared to traditional casting, which has far more micro cavities in the metal.

The history of UFIP would not be complete without mentioning the collaboration of UFIP with the percussionist, Andrea Centazzo. During the 1970s, he developed the ICTUS 75 range of cast percussion instruments, the most famous (and most copied) being the 'Icebell'. Other instruments the he invented were:-

TAMTAM – large, heavy bronze lens shaped gongs from 8"/20cm to 38"/96cm diameter. These were the forerunner of the Targo tam-tams.

OGORORO BELLS – small, tuned, flat discs in a set of eight.

SHENG – heavy flat discs from 10"/25cm to 13"/33cm, tuned in a pentatonic series

TAMPANG – an unlathed chinese cymbal suspended from the edge in 16"/41cm to 24"/60cm diameters

LOKOLE – lathed flat discs with the 'bending' sound of chinese opera gongs

BURMA BELL – 5 different copies of a Burmese Kyeezee

SYMPHONIC GONG – heavy, cast gong looking like a cross between a bossed gong and an abstract sculpture

BELL TREE – small bronze cups mounted one above the other in an ascending size.

The current range of UFIP gongs and tam-tams are made from either cast bronze or from rolled sheets of bronze or brass. Hence they transcend both the European tradition of forming gongs from sheet metal and the Far East tradition of casting. They also use (or have used) several alloys – B20, B12 and B8 bronze and, surprisingly, brass! Generally, instruments up to 28"/71cm in diameter are made from bronze and from 32"/81cm diameter from brass. Forming the gongs from either casting or from rolled metal sheets involves hammering as well as lathing techniques. The cast gongs are sub-contracted back to one of the founding families who specialise in bell casting, the sheet metal gongs being made at the factory. Rotocasting is not used for gong making at present as the gong sizes are beyond the current capabilities of the machines. As ever, the gong smiths are highly skilled artisans constantly tuning the instruments with expert hammer blows. The artisan history of Tuscany shows itself in the casting techniques;- chemical balance, the right heat and the evenness of the pour. Once created, the instruments themselves are rested for two months before shipping to distributers and customers.

Before describing the current (2012) range of gongs and tam-tams, I should mention the 'VIBRA' tam-tams that were available in the 70s and 80s. These were made by the Zanchi family who are part of UFIP but sold cymbals and tam-tams under the 'VIBRA' trade name to dealers in the USA and UK. The VIBRA tam-tams then formed the core of the 'Targo' tam-tam range (see section 4.2.2).

Prior to 2010, UFIP gongs and tam-tams were divided into two distinct ranges: The 'Targo' tam-tam range and the 'ART' gong range. However, the distinction between gong and tam-tam was not as clear cut as the nomenclature would seem to indicate. Some of the ART gong range are actually tam-tams while the lack of a turned over edge and rim to some of the instruments in the 'Targo' range has resulted in the misbelief by some that <u>all</u> tam-tams are flat gongs without a rim.

4.2.2 Targo Tam-tams

Targo Circular

A slightly convex flat gong with no rim or turned over edge. It has concentric lathed circular marks radiating out from the face similar to a Wuhan 'Sun' gong. The face was also lightly hammered. They were made from cast B20 bronze and available in 3 sizes – 20"/50cm, 24"/60cm and 28"/70cm. The finish was usually a bright gold. The tone is a warm crash and shimmer, even from *pianissimo* strokes. There is a strong overall fundamental note with a prolonged sustain and a hidden whistle. The crash is warm but not overpowering and is reasonably long lasting. They have a lot more depth of sound than the equivalent Wuhan wind gongs and different tones and harmonics can be found when playing the various rings with harder beaters. Overall they have a very pleasing sound and are worthy of further investigation. The gong is a bit small for big orchestral crashes, but more than suitable for pit/theatre work and very suitable for sound healing, especially for those with small treatment rooms or close neighbours!

Targo Thin Hammered

This was made from a thinner gauge metal than the Targo Circular and doesn't have the concentric patterned circles, but was lathed and had random hammer marks across its surface. It was slightly convex in form and without a rim. This gong looked and sounded very much like the Wuhan 'wind' gongs. The harmonics washed over each other very readily as it was a responsive instrument. Best played *pianissimo* to *mezzo forte* as the *forte* crash decays very quickly. It was only available in a 28"/70cm diameter.

Targo Border Hammered

This was a very interesting design – it had a shallow convex face but is surrounded by a prominent border that turns back on itself to form a rim. Striking the face gave a much more focussed sound which was clear and loud. Striking towards the edge gave a much more explosive impact. Again, it was only available in a 28"/70cm diameter.

4.2.3 'ART' Gongs and Tam-tams

ART I (tam-tam)

Convex-shaped gong without a rim or boss resembling an ancient Greek shield. It had a heavily hammered face and sometimes had vertical scrape marks on the face. It was available in several different sizes and two different metals:-

20"/51cm, 24"/61cm and 28"/71cm diameters in rolled B8 bronze

32"/81cm, 36"/91cm, 40"/102cm and 52"/132cm diameters in rolled brass.

ART II (tam-tam)

Similar to the Targo Border tam-tam i.e. very shallow convex centre with a prominent border and rim. The border and rim was heavily hammered with a few light hammered tuning strokes around the face. It was available as:-

20"/51cm, 24"/61cm and 28"/71cm diameters in rolled B8 bronze

32"/81cm, 36"/91cm and 40"/102cm diameters in rolled brass

The ART II B8 had similar sound characteristics to a small Chao gong and was more like a tam-tam than a tuned gong though there is an element of tuning – 24" versions were thought to be tuned to E3 or F3 though other tunings have been reported. The ART II brass gong shares many similarities to the ART I brass tam-tams, with a low fundamental but a bit more body leaning towards the Paiste Symphonic Gong sound, although the sustain was not that long.

ART III (tam-tam)

As the ART II gong but with a much more heavily, random hammered face with the result that it looked like the Paiste 'Earth' Sound Creation Gong. Available sizes were:-

20"/51cm, 24"/61cm and 28"/71cm diameters in rolled B8 bronze

32"/81cm, 36"/91cm and 40"/102cm diameters in rolled brass.

The sound was earthy and warm, giving a deep boom slightly Chinese in character. It can splash like a tam-tam but the sustain is not that long.

ART IV (tuned gong)

Not as heavily hammered as the ART III and the hammer marks are much more uniform. In addition, the centre was hammered out into a boss. Available sizes were:-

20"/51cm, 24"/61cm and 28"/71cm diameters in rolled B8 bronze

32"/81cm, 36"/91cm and 40"/102cm diameters in rolled brass.

Similar in character to a 'worn' Paiste Tuned Gong in that there is a definite tuned note (E2 has been suggested for a 24" version) with a low frequency vibration but more splashy overtones when reaching *mezzo forte*.

ART V (tuned gong)

Similar in appearance to the ART IV gong but less hammering and the flat face around the central boss was un-hammered. It had a bright bell-like sound (like a small Thai gong) but gave some shimmer when struck *forte*. Available sizes were:-

20"/51cm, 24"/61cm and 28"/71cm diameters in rolled B8 bronze

32"/81cm, 36"/91cm and 40"/102cm diameters in rolled brass.

4.2.4 Current Range (2012)

Cast Bronze tam-tams (tam-tams Bronzo Fuso)

Essentially the 'Targo' tam-tam, available in 20"/50cm, 24"/60cm, and 28"/70 cm diameters with sound characteristics as described for the main Targo tam-tam in section 4.2.2. These really are superb instruments for the price and deserve more recognition outside of their native homeland of Italy and beyond UFIP aficionados such as Ed Mann in the USA and myself in the UK. Ed has made the comment that the casting and hammering process incorporates many techniques used in bell, cymbal and gong making (though not the rotocasting method) and for him at least, these gongs are part bell, part cymbal and part gong, which gives them their unique sonic presence.

UFIP Cast B20 bronze tam-tam
(also known as a 'Targo' tam-tam)

UFIP Sheet B8 bronze tam-tam in the
'Tiger' finish

Sheet Bronze tam-tams (tam-tams B8 Laminato, Finitura Tradiz, Finitura Tiger).

A range of tam-tams (which appear to be the ex-ART I sheet bronze models) made from sheet B8 bronze and of the same cross-section as the Targo tam-tam i.e. a slight convex shape with no turned over edge or central boss. The sound is not as strong or as sustained as the 'Targo' and the crash is short-lived, which reflects the different tonal qualities of B8 bronze compared to B20 bronze. They sound a bit like a large 'ride' cymbal, (one could argue that visually they are a little like a 'flat ride' cymbal) – not good for large crashes but nevertheless pleasing in their own way. I use one for adding a bit of splash when larger gongs are being played as a 'drone'. Again, not overpowering, but useful in enclosed spaces or small rooms. The overall tone is lighter than the B20 cast bronze tam-tam.

They are available in two finishes – a plain yellowy bronze 'traditional' finish, and the visually striking 'Tiger' finish. With a 'Tiger' finish, an orange coloured lacquer is applied which is patterned using scrapers, emery paper and gas torches. The finish is a stripy, wavy pattern representing aspects of a tiger, though personally, the pattern is reminiscent of those glass ionised plasma balls which emit a 'lightning' effect when touched. There is a definite visual impact, but the surface is distressed and if you want a scratch-free gong, this finish is not for you. Available in available in 20"/50cm, 24"/60cm, and 28"/70 cm diameters.

Sheet Brass Tam-tams (Tam-tams Ottone Laminato)

These instruments have the same cross-section as the two previous tam-tams (flat convex, no rim, no boss), but with a heavily hammered face and are made from brass sheet with a clear lacquer coating. As with the tam-tams described above, they appear to be the old brass ART I gongs. I approached these gongs with a degree of scepticism – brass has only ever been used for budget cymbals in the West and they sounded little better than the proverbial dustbin lid. I was however, completely taken aback by the sound of a 32"/80cm model I bought recently that gives a completely unexpected and pleasing sound. It has a wonderful low growl of a crash with good sustain and overlapping harmonics that sound like someone strumming their fingers over the lower strings of a grand piano. It has a certain weight to the sound which is more 'oriental' than other Western gongs and the roar is warm without sounding shrill. The fundamental note booms with those supporting bass piano string tones. Other UFIP gong users say that they appear to improve with age. I haven't had mine long enough to categorically say this is true, but it does appear to be changing slightly (in a good way) from when I first bought it. Additionally, use of a flumi on it is remarkably easy, setting up all sorts of weird and wonderful sounds.

This gong has its roots in the brass ART I gong range, though without the vertical scrape marks and the available sizes (32"/80cm, 36"/90cm, 40"/100cm, 44"/110cm, 48"/120cm and 52"/130cm diameters) make them serious contenders for orchestral tam-tams. The 52"/130cm diameter model is reputedly 4mm thick. If you are still not sure, look at the price – the smaller diameters are no more than two-thirds the price of their Paiste equivalent and the larger diameters are about half the price. They are considered good enough for the likes of the La Scala Opera's orchestra in Milan and the Metropolitan Orchestra in New York and I have heard a rumour that the Vienna Philharmonic uses them as well.

UFIP sheet brass tam-tam

There is, however, one draw back with the 'tam-tam' range. The gongs are suspended using thin chord. When the gongs are struck with any force, they tend to pivot where the chord passes through the gong near to the edge. This has the effect of dampening the instrument as the top of the gong touches the hanging chord. I have tried substituting this chord with the gut chord used by Paiste. As this material is stiffer, there is less pivoting of the gong about the hanging hole and the gong tends to swing more on the stand suspension hooks. Unfortunately, a loud stroke on the gongs usually results in the rim of the gong touching the gut and a nasty buzzing sound accompanying the gong sound.

Gongs – Sheet Bronze with Border (Gongs B8 Bronzo Laminato)

The gongs share physical and acoustical similarities with the old ART II B8 gong. They are available in 20"/50cm, 24"/60cm and 28"/70cm sizes.

Gongs – Sheet Bronze with Bell and Border (Gongs B8 Bronzo Laminato con Campana)

These gongs share physical and acoustical similarities to the ART V B8 gong. Available in 20"/50cm, 24"/60cm and 28"/70cm sizes. There is a strong element of tuning within the gong but it cannot be ordered tuned to a specific pitch.

Gongs – Sheet Brass Symphonic with Border (Gongs Ottone Laminato)

These gongs share physical and acoustical similarities with the ART II brass gongs. They are available in 32"/80cm, 36"/90cm and 40"/100cm sizes.

Sheet brass symphonic gong with border/ ART II brass gong (Courtesy of Ed Mann)

UFIP have also produced cast B20 bronze tuned gongs in a range known as 'Genovese'. They are said to have weighed 15kg and the entire shape, including the rim and boss, was cast, then lathed down to the correct proportions. This contrasts with both Paiste and South-East Asian tuned gongs where the boss and rim are formed by hammering.

4.3   SABIAN

4.3.1   Background

Sabian are one of the three largest cymbal manufactures in the world. It was founded by Robert Zildjian in 1981 after he had parted company with his brother Armand, both of whom had inherited the Zildjian Cymbal Company from their father Armand some two years previously. Hence the art of cymbal making at Sabian can be traced back some 350 years to its cymbal making ancestors in Constantinople (modern Istanbul).

Robert Zildjian took over the Zildjian's satellite plant in Meductic, New Brunswick in Canada where he initially concentrated on making high quality orchestral cymbals, this being his foremost love. He knew that Sabian had to establish itself as a high quality musical instrument maker in its own right, rather than rely on previous associations. This hand hammered (HH) range of cymbals swept the orchestral world by storm and they are my preferred cymbal – I have three pairs and three suspended cymbals in my collection.

When it comes to gongs, Sabian also make their own as well as importing Chao and Wind gongs from China. The factory-made gongs consist of a Symphonic Gong (based on the old Zildjian 'Turkish' gong) and a Zodiac gong with metals and manufacturing techniques similar to European practice. The Chao gongs are being offered to satisfy the North American preference for these gongs over European tam-tams.

4.3.2 'Zodiac' Gong *(tam-tam)*

The Zodiac Gong has been developed with percussionists and sound healers in mind. The Zodiac Gong encompasses all 12 signs of the Zodiac in one gong rather than a range of 12 individual gongs, though it would be interesting to see such a range being developed. It is available in four sizes – 22"/56cm, 24"/61cm, 26"/66cm and 28"/71cm. They are made from Nickel Silver in a formula of 70% copper, 25% zinc and 5% nickel making it a 'true' nickel silver alloy. Sabian describes the manufacture as being in the style of 'the classic European school'.

The gong is flat faced with an angular rim (approx. 45 degrees to the face of the gong). The centre of the gong is plain but has interesting lathing and hammer marks radiating out from this centre to the edge.

The colour of the gong is a natural brass/gold effect, with the Sabian logo and 'Zodiac Gong' printed on the face. Sabian describes the sound as a 'warm, focussed fundamental with rich sustaining overtones'. It has a very definite splash/punchy primary sound with washing overtones and a rapid decay. In my opinion it is better played *piano* to *mezzo forte* for a warmer sound. Any louder than this and it is quite brash. This gong is also available in an unbranded form (28"/71cm diameter) and known as a 'Conference' gong.

Sabian Zodiac Gong
(courtesy of Sabian)

4.3.3 Symphonic Gong *(tam-tam)*

This gong is based on the old Turkish Gong made by Zildjian before the brothers split. Turkish is an apt name as the making of the gong has much in common with the way cymbals are manufactured. It is flat faced with the same angular rim as the Zodiac Gong. It is lathed on both sides from the centre outwards, though the original Zildjian Turkish Gong had a hole drilled in the centre just like a cymbal. It is made from bronze – the classic 80% copper, 20% tin formula. The Sabian version has a black centre and black rim in the style of a Chao gong with the Sabian logo and 'Symphonic Gong' printed on the face. It has been modified

*Sabian Symphonic Gong
(courtesy of Sabian)*

somewhat from the original Turkish Gong with an increase in weight and thickness to improve the response. It is available in 24"/61cm, 26"/66cm and 28"/71cm sizes.

The sound consists of a strong fundamental with washing overtones giving a rounded warm response when played *piano* to *forte*. Beyond this the sound becomes a bit brash but the decay lasts longer than the Zodiac Gong.

4.3.4 Chinese Gong *(tam-tam)*

The Sabian Chinese Gong is essentially a Chao gong made in the Wuhan area of China and Sabian selects them carefully. They receive some cosmetic enhancements when they arrive at the factory such as re-branding with the Sabian logo and 'Chinese Gong' print. The centre and edge black colourings are more uniform than a 'raw' Chinese Chao gong. The metal is bronze-based on a formula of approximately 76% copper, 22% tin, 1% zinc and traces of iron. They are available in 30"/76cm, 34"/86cm and 40"/102cm diameters. Sabian describe the sound as 'a definite primary impact response followed by an outpouring of raw dark overtones. Full sounding'.

4.3.5 Wind Gong *(tam-tam)*

The 2010 Sabian product list indicates that a 22"/55cm Wind Gong is available. This is very similar to other wind gongs produced in China with a hand-hammered unlathed surface. It speaks quickly when played and has a warm dark response. The version I have seen did not have a Sabian logo on it.

4.4 ZILDJIAN

4.4.1 Background

The Avedis Zildjian Company is well known to just about every drummer and percussionist. One of the world's largest cymbal manufacturers, it produces a very wide range of cymbals covering almost every genre of music from classical to jazz to rock, plus everything in between.

Their cymbal making ancestry dates back to 17th century Constantinople when, in 1623, an Armenian alchemist named Avedis discovered a way to alloy 8 parts copper to 2 parts tin in such a way that the metal could be used to make thin cymbals (or 'zils') without becoming brittle. This 'secret' (believed to be in the melting and mixing process) was passed down through the family for generations. By 1908 Avedis III had emigrated to America, and in 1929 cymbal production had started at a small plant in Norfolk Downs, Massachusetts (MA). Following a fire, another plant was set up in North Quincy MA and the company expanded, helped by the growing interest in jazz at that time. The modern factory at Norwell MA was set up in 1972.

The gongs sold by Zildjian have either been made in house or imported from the Far East and re-branded. The range has changed over the years; during the 1980's, it consisted of four gong types – 'Turkish', 'Gamelan', 'Taiwan' and 'Chinese'. The current range comprises a number of different types sourced from China (see Section 4.4.3).

4.4.2 Previous Range of Gongs

Turkish Gong (tam-tam)

This gong had a flat face with lathing and hammering very similar to their cast cymbals (such as the 'K' series), with a small hole in the centre from the lathe spindle. The edge was turned over at an angle of about 45 degrees. They were designed for orchestral and symphonic users although they were a bit small for large orchestras. They were available in 22"/56cm, 24"/61cm, 26"/66cm and 28"/71cm diameters. They had a mellow sound, a rapid 'crash' and a long sustain.

Gamelan Gong (tuned gong)

At first glance, these gongs looked very much like a cymbal with a cup and sloping face which was lathed and hammered. It was made from a far heavier gauge metal so when struck on the boss/cup, it gave out a dark rich bell like sound similar to its namesake, with a long sustain. They were not, however, tuned to a particular pitch. They were available in 20"/51cm and 22"/56cm diameters.

Chinese Gong (tam-tam)

Very similar in appearance and sound to a 'Wind' gong – fast response crash and decay. Only available in 18"/46cm diameter.

Taiwan Gong (tam-tam)

These were made in Taiwan especially for Zildjian. They were mainly sheet bronze with vertical scrape marks, but with a black centre and rim like a Chao gong on which they were based. They 'spoke' very quickly with a faster decay than would be expected for their size. They were available in 30"/76cm, 34"/86cm, 40"/102cm and 48"/122cm diameters.

4.4.3 Current (2011) range of gongs

The current range of gongs are essentially carefully selected and re-branded gongs from the Wuhan area of China. A fuller description of the original gong types can be found in the 'Wuhan' section (Section 4.5) but the 2011 range was as follows:-

Bao Gong – A 10"/25cm bossed gong with a bell like tone when struck on the boss.

Tam-Tam Gong (Opera Gong) – 10"/25cm gong, lathed front and rear with a clear tone and upward *glissando* when struck. It is not clear why they chose the nomenclature 'tam-tam gong' as they are not what most people think of as a tam-tam. Most confusing!

Jing Gong (Opera Gong) – 12"/30cm larger version of the tam-tam gong but with a bright tone and downward *glissando* when struck.

Fuyin Gong – 15"/38cm gong, rich sounding wash and duration.

Wind Gong – as previous Wind (Chinese) gong but now available in 24"/61cm diameter.

Chinese Gong – essentially a Chao gong. Available in 26"/66cm, 30"/76cm, 34"/86cm and 40"/102cm diameters.

Zildjian Bao gong

Zildjian Chinese Gong

4.5   CHINESE GONGS AND 'WUHAN'

4.5.1 Background

China has a long history of gong- and cymbal-making dating back nearly 2,000 years. Forges could be found all over the country, but most were concentrated around areas of copper deposits. Today, the biggest concentration of gong makers can be found around the city of Wuhan in the province of Hubei.

Cymbals and gongs have been exported from China for many hundreds of years, either to sellers of Chinese products or, more recently, to Western musical instrument manufacturers or distributors who often re-brand the gongs with their own logos, sometimes making it impossible to trace a gong's origins. This is not the only hurdle in trying to research gong-making in China. Different companies often use different names for the same gong type, they refer to 'brass' percussion instruments when they are made from bronze (or vice-versa) and they are often part of a larger company that may make copper and brass pots and pans, or even tractors and other agricultural machinery!

The main issue with modern Chinese gongs is that of quality. Many are mass- produced and gongs of the same type and diameter can sound remarkably different. I have played Chao gongs of a similar size that, no matter what size beater is used, just go 'bong', while others 'speak' so quickly that they sound like breaking glass. There are also reports that recycled copper wire and tin are used in the production of some gongs which introduce impurities into the molten metal. Don't be put off by these seemingly negative aspects, however, there are some truly wonderful sounding Chinese gongs. My advice is to find yourself a good dealer who can source and select high quality gongs from the manufacturers on your behalf.

When the name 'Wuhan' is used in this book, it is referring to a number of manufacturers producing gongs in this area, or are using this name in their title, rather than one particular company that brands its gongs and cymbals as 'Wuhan'. It is Chinese custom and practice to use the city, province or town in their titles. My research has shown at least three manufacturers following this practice: the Wuhan Golden Bird Fine Gong Manufacturing Co. Ltd, the Wuhan Haiping Musical Instrument Manufacturing Co. Ltd, and the Hubei Fotma Machinery Company which, I believe, is affiliated to Wuhan Haiping as they use the same 'WH xxx' product codes.

Wuhan Golden Bird is the oldest of the above named manufacturers. Their gong lineage can be traced back 1900 years. The Gaojiahe Gong Factory was established in 1909, when there were some 300 coppersmiths in Wuhan. During the Cultural Revolution it had to change its name to the city in which it was located. Over recent years the original name has come back into use (as well as the name 'Gaohongtai) and some of its products are branded 'Wuhan'. The company claims four generations of gong makers, and is looking to enhance the skills of other gong makers throughout the country, as well as establishing closer links with musicians etc in the West. Much of their output is exported to the USA as well as elsewhere and they claim to have the biggest range of Chinese percussion instruments manufactured from copper-based metals – some 180 specifications. The website for the city of Wuhan states that gongs can be bought from the Gaohongtai Factory and give examples of some of the larger gongs produced e.g a 53"/135cm Chao gong for the Berlin Symphony Orchestra and a pair of 56"/142 cm Chao gongs for an orchestra in Japan and for the factory itself.

Wuhan Haiping was founded in 1984. It is a large facility with an output of some 200 tonnes of musical instruments. Their range consists of some 20 types of gong, 10 types of cymbals, plus bells and other instruments across 150 specifications. Sometimes their gongs bear the 'Eastsound' logo.

Hubei Fotma Machinery Co. also make gongs and other instruments amongst their products alongside tungsten carbide tools, construction machinery and tractors. They claim over thirty years of experience in 'brass' percussion manufacturing. The gongs and cymbals are occasionally branded 'Jiayin' and sometimes 'Eastsound' which is a brand used by Wuhan Haiping. The similarity of their website (www.china-gong.com) to that of Wuhan Haiping (www.chinagong.com) and the similar product line up and product code indicates that the companies are closely related. Just to add a bit more confusion, during my research I discovered another firm marketing Wuhan gongs. This is Xingsir Music (www.wuhangong.com) who market the same range as Wuhan Haiping using the same product codes!

The 'WHxxx' code has been listed next to the gongs described below where it has been identified that the same code is being used by at least two distributers, in order to try and avoid confusion.

4.5.2 Chao Gong (WH007) *(tam-tam)*

Probably the oldest lineage of gongs available today and probably the most numerous. The Chao (also spelt Chau) gong is very popular with the majority of the world's symphony orchestras, especially in the United States, as well as some of the big name orchestras in Europe e.g. the Berlin Philharmonic. The Chao gong is instantly recognisable with its black or dark brown centre and colouring around the edge of the face of the gong, with a shiny gold coloured mid band separating the two. This patterning gives it another name – the Bulls Eye Gong. It is also referred to as a 'Chinese' gong by both Zildjian and Sabian and as a 'Tam-tam Gong' by Stagg. Many orchestral percussionists refer to it as a 'Wuhan tam-tam' which recognises the city in China where the vast majority of these gongs are made today.

The earliest Chao gong was discovered in a tomb at the Guixian site in the Guangxi Zhuany Autonomous region of China. It dates from the early Western Han Dynasty (approx. 200 BC – AD 220).

The gongs are made from cast bronze to a formula of approximately 76% copper to 23% tin plus traces of zinc and iron. The molten bronze is poured into sand or clay moulds, allowed to cool, then is repeatedly hammered and re-heated to form a disk with a shallow rim and shallow convex face. Next the gong is lathed both front and rear between the centre and rim bands to remove the black or brown copper oxide formed as part of the casting process. Then the gong is tuned with further hammering before it is finally polished. This final hammering varies in size and depth and you can also find the occasional gouge or cut marks as quality control is not always rigorous. Being of cast construction, the gongs have a certain brittleness and will crack or shatter if dropped onto a hard unyielding surface. They are also very heavy. My 40"/100 cm Chao gong weighs 45 pounds (20 kg)! The sizes range from about 10"/25 cm to 51"/130 cm in 2"/5 cm increments to about 40"/100 cm diameter then in 4"/10 cm increments beyond that. Both Golden Bird and Haiping have made gongs from 60"/150 cm to 72"/180 cm in diameter, which must weigh a colossal amount!

The sound characteristics of a Chao gong are what most people describe as 'Chinese', which probably comes from their use in film scores describing oriental scenes rather than a sound that can only be found in China. Like the Paiste Symphonic Gong, the Chao, when struck *piano*, has a very strong fundamental note though some harmonics and overtones shimmer quietly over the top. Being a cast gong, hence thicker metal than a Paiste Symphonic Gong, the depth of tone is much lower size for size. I often liken this to a 'dragon snoring' when describing this sound on the larger instruments. This penetrating *piano* or *pianissimo* tone makes them preferable, in my opinion, for orchestral works where the tam-tam is required to chime away quietly to itself as in the third movement of Mahler's Symphony No.1 or the 'Russian Easter Festival Overture' by Rimsky-Korsakov.

When played *forte* or *fortissimo*, the crash is much more immediate with lots of overtones, but decays away very quickly. There is also a certain jangling sound within the gong, almost as if the metal crystals are free to move within the skin of the gong. This is probably due to the crystal lattice not being as compressed as that found in rolled sheet bronze. It is because of this short lived crash and decay, which is not consistent between equivalent sized gongs, that they are less suitable for the big *fortissimo* crashes at the end of Mahler's Symphonies No.2 and No.8 (which for me can spoil the entire performance) but does make them suitable for several *fortissimo* strokes that follow each other in quick succession or where the sound needs to be controlled more. Examples include Britten's War Requiem, and Respighi's *Pines of Rome*. The decay sound of the Chao also has a distinctive throbbing that is very pleasant and adds to the musical quality in a classical music piece if the rest of the orchestra has quietened down sufficiently for this to come through. Most of the time, though, this deep fundamental cannot be heard when orchestras are playing loud, except by the percussion section, which I think colours some player's views on the relative merits of Paiste tam-tams versus Chao tam-tams.

Chinese Chao Gong

For sound healers, the Chao gong makes a very good 'Earth' gong – the word 'earthy' describing the sound very effectively. They make good alternatives to the Paiste Sound Creation Earth gongs, especially considering the price! They are also very useful as an alternative to the Paiste Symphonic Gong as they produce a wide range of tones and harmonics, though some would say they are less pure than the Symphonic Gong.

There are also several variants of the Chao gong that are currently marketed by Gongs Unlimited in the USA. The 'Sub Atomic' gong has four concentric rings of alternating lathed and unlathed metal across its face (unlathed centre). The lathed areas are polished. The 'Tesla' gong is a completely unlathed Chao gong with a low dark tone. The 'Dark Star' gong is similar, but with a lathed and polished centre spot and, again, a dark tone with little crash. The 'Chocolate Drop' gong has an unlathed centre but the rest of the gong is lathed and polished.

4.5.3 Wind and Sun Gongs (WH015) *(tam-tam)*

Another popular Chinese gong is the 'Wind' gong. It is sometimes known as a 'Feng' gong though one Chinese firm uses the term 'Feng' for another type of gong.

The Wind gong is essentially a flat gong, though it can be slightly convex like a flat shield, or it can be flat across most of the face but with a very shallow slope at the edges. It has no rim. The gong is normally cast into a pancake shaped mass and then beaten very thin though there are rolled sheet versions. They are mostly made from B20 bronze though M63 brass is also used. They are fully lathed front and rear and are extensively hammered.

There is a moderate fundamental note but the main characteristics of this instrument are the washing overtones and harmonics, crashing highs and brilliant shimmer that give this gong its name – a rushing wind through the bamboo groves. Smaller instruments (7"/18 cm to 12"/30 cm) have a more bell-like tone due to the thickness of the metal. The sizes available are 6"/15cm to 39"/100cm in 2"/5 cm increments and 43"/110cm to 60"/150 cm diameters in 4"/10cm increments.

They are rarely seen in orchestras as the fundamental note does not penetrate enough and the crash can be a bit too trashy for symphonic works. They occasionally find favour with rock groups as an accompaniment to the similar sounding 'Chinese' cymbal and with the pit orchestra in a theatre. By careful placement of the microphone, there is no need to rely on its own power to cut through the mass of sound at a rock gig. Where these gongs have found a major following is in sound therapy, feng shui, space clearing, yoga and other 'New Age' practices. The portability of even the larger sizes (24" to 32") makes them easy to walk with and carry round various rooms of the house or around a person's body, sounding the gong as you go. The cost is also a big factor in their favour when compared to Chao or Paiste gongs.

Related to the Wind gong is the 'Sun' gong. The physical appearance is similar to the Wind gong – essentially flat face with slightly sloping edges or slightly convex. However, the faces are not fully lathed. Instead, circular bands of unlathed areas radiate out from the centre of the gong. These unlathed areas give a certain depth to the sound, richer overtones and melodically more complex so the essential characteristic is a cross over between the Wind and Chao gongs, both in sound and price. They can also be very grounding. Available in at least 20"/50cm to 35"/90cm in 10cm steps.

Chinese Wind (Feng) gong

4.5.4 Chinese 'Tuned' Gongs

Surprisingly, given that it is surrounded by countries producing a wealth of different sized tuned gongs, China has little in the way of tuned gongs. What exists is quite small and has been developed to be hand held like many of their gongs. They are mainly used as musical accompaniments to operas, plays and street theatre. Some are considered a sacred gong and are used in temples.

Bao Gong (WH008)

Bao gongs have a raised central boss within a gently sloping face and a reasonably deep rim. They can be obtained fully lathed and polished, partially lathed (e.g. just the central boss), or unfinished with just the black copper oxide coating. They are made from cast bronze and are lightly hammered. They are offered in sizes from 11"/27cm to 24"/60cm in 5cm steps with 12"/30cm, 14"/35cm, 16"/40cm and 18"/45cm being the most common. There are also several designs. Some have a shallow valley towards the edge of the face before turning over into a deep 2" to 3" rim. The gongs are made from slightly thicker gauge metal that gives an overall bell- like sound with subtle overtones and a long decay. The gongs are not normally tuned to any Western scales but 'Dream Gongs and Cymbals' offer a range of tuned gongs based on the Bao to order.

Gou Gong

Similar in style to the Bao gong but with a larger diameter central boss. Also made from bronze and available in lathed and polished, semi-lathed and polished, or black oxide finishes. Available in one size of 6"/15cm, they are available in sets of six, each tuned to a slightly different pitch.

'Planet' Gongs

A new departure for one of the Wuhan companies is the production of five planet gongs with tunings based on Hans Coustos' work, though pitched an octave above. They each have a central dome/boss which is the same size on both diameters available, an almost flat surrounding face and a turned over rim which is reasonably deep (3/4" – 1") for their size. They are lightly hand hammered (though there is some evidence of machine hammering and bending, especially around the rim) and are available in a plain oxide finish (9"/24cm gongs) or lathed and polished (7"/18cm gongs). The larger sizes appear cast, though the smaller sizes look to be made from sheet bronze. The Planets available are:-

Planet	Size	Tuning (Hz)	Nearest note
Venus	7"/18cm	442.46	A4
Jupiter	7"/18cm	367.46	F # 4
Saturn	9"/23cm	295.70	D4
Mars	9"/23cm	289.44	D4
Mercury	9"/23cm	282.54	C # 4

Wuhan Planet Gongs

Opera Gongs (WH001)

Although lacking the bossed centre of regular tuned gongs (the shape is a flat centre, sloping surrounding face and shallow rim, similar to the 'hand' gongs in the next section), the unique tonal qualities of these gongs require inclusion in this section. When struck, the initial impact sound is a bright clear tone. However a hard or repeated strike is then followed by a sharp and highly unusual rise or fall in pitch. The size of the gong is not necessarily an indicator of which way the pitch will 'bend' or *glissando* (slide up or down).

These gongs are used in Chinese opera to announce main characters or punctuate aspects of the story. The larger gongs with a descending tone are used to announce male roles, major characters and dramatic points. The smaller gong with an ascending pitch are used to announce women, minor characters and points of humour or mirth. The sound is very dramatic but short lived.

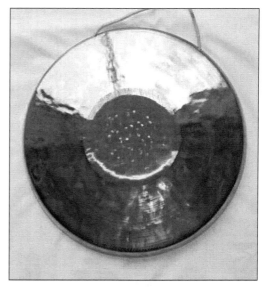

Chinese Opera Gong

The gongs are normally made from bronze (though brass is also used), lathed on both sides for a bright finish and hammered, mainly on the central flat face with some lighter hammer marks on the sloping sides. They are normally available as a pair mounted in an aluminium or steel frame, one gong having an ascending pitch, one having a descending pitch. When mounted this way, the larger gong is some 2"/5cm bigger than the other gong. Sizes that are normally available are 8"/20cm, 10"/25cm, 12"/30cm, 13"/33cm, and 14"/36cm. They are also known as 'Jing' or 'Jing Bao' gongs after the opera in Beijing.

4.5.5 'Hand Held' gongs

In this section a range of gongs have been grouped together under a generic heading of 'Hand Held' – small gongs normally held in one hand for playing. They are often associated with Chinese theatre and lion, dog and dragon dances. These gongs often look and sound very similar, with the diameter of the instrument resulting in a different name as well as the gong's use in a certain piece of theatre or dance.

It has not been possible to listen to every gong type described here, however where a sound or tone is not described, it can be reasonably assumed to fit the known sounds and tones which can be bright clear and bell-like, crashy and warm like a tam-tam, or even a combination of the two.

There are two basic shapes to these gongs. One has a flat central section with the rest of the face gently sloping down to a shallow rim. The flat central section varies in diameter and often has an effect on the gong's sound character. For reference, this has been called 'Design A'. The other has a flat face which turns over into a deep rim which has been called 'Design B'. All are made from bronze though there are some brass versions.

Tiger Gong (Hu Yan Gong) (WH003)

Visually very similar to the Opera Gong, it is Design A, lathed on both sides with a bright finish. It is hammered front and rear with a lot of hammering on the front centre section. The rim appears to be turned over using a machine rather than from hammering. The central section is wider than that found on an Opera Gong – nominally 7"/18cm on a 14"/36cm model.

Light strokes in the centre produce a clear tone with a long sustain. Heavier strokes bring out crashier sounds and overtones but the fundamental still sustains through. There is also a slight *glissando*, mostly descending, but occasionally ascending. Strokes on the outer face produce the same trashier tones with a long sustain. The sound is meant to imitate the roar of a tiger, hence the gong's name.

Sizes available are 12"/30cm (treble), 13"/33cm (treble), 14"/36cm (alto), 15"/38cm (bass).

A related version is the 'Hui Yin' Gong from Jiangsu Province (WH006). These are slightly smaller than the normal Tiger gongs, having fewer overtones. They are available in 8.5"/21.5cm treble, 8.5"/21.5cm alto and 9"/22.5cm bass sounds.

Pasi Gong (WH130)

The Pasi Gong can come in various forms, nominally conforming to Design A but with a very small diameter centre section or with no flat centre, just a very shallow cone. They are usually lathed on both sides and are heavily hammered. The sound is a bright bell-like sound with simmering overtones, but it gets crashier in character when struck harder. There is a long sustain. They are used to announce the start of a performance or signal the use of 'magic' in the performance. Available in 10"/26cm, 12"/30cm and 15"/38cm.

White Gong/Smooth Gong (WH004)

This gong is the flatest of the gongs made to Design A. Lathed front and rear for a bright finish and heavily hammered. The smaller gongs have a mellow bell-like tone with some shimmer when struck hard. The decay is fairly short. Some of the larger gongs e.g. 22"/56 cm in diameter can sound like a Chao gong. Available in 12"/30cm, 14"/37cm, 16"/40cm, 18"/45cm, 20"/50cm and 24"/60cm. These are the largest of the hand gongs.

Xiang Jin/ Jia Gong (WH009)

A small hand gong to Design B – i.e. a flat face with deep rim, made from bronze. The brown/black copper oxide coating is not removed and a diamond pattern is scraped onto this surface. Normally played with a small wooden stick to give a 'clang' like sound and often used as a more rhythmical accompaniment in theatre and lion/dragon dances. It can also give a roaring crash when required. Available in 8"/20cm to 24"/60 cm diameters in 2"/5 cm steps.

Dan Da Gong (Chuan Gong) (WH011)

A very simple gong to Design B and similar to the Xiang Jia gong except that there is no decoration at all, just a plain cast bronze gong, hammered but not lathed. Probably the simplest gong available from China. Available in 6"/15cm and 7"/18.5cm sizes.

Night Gong

Also related to the Dan Da and Xiang Jia gongs, the Night Gong has the flat face and deep rim of Design B. There is no lathing or scraping of the metal, but the face is heavily hammered in a similar way to some of the Paiste Sound Creation gongs. The sound is a darker bell–like tone with some top end shimmer and some slight 'bend' or *glissando* to the note. Only one size is available – 17"/44cm.

Yun Gong (WH020)

A very small gong to Design B but with lathed front and rear and a deep rim. Available in 4"/10cm or 5"/12cm.

Ma Gong (WH210)

Gong to Design A with lathed front and rear faces but a slightly deeper rim with some hammering. It has a mid bell–like tone with little shimmer unless struck hard when it can sound a bit sharp. Sizes – 6.5"/17cm and 8"/20cm.

Other Hand Gongs

The following are all small hand gongs mainly to Design A with lathed front and rear faces and various degrees of hammering. Available from Wuhan Haiping, though some are sold by Stagg under the Opera Gong heading in their 2010 catalogue.

'Hand Gong'(WH006) – 8.5"/21.5cm in High, Medium or Low tones.

'Xiang Xiao' Gong (WH109) – 9"/22cm.

'Wu' or 'Fong' or 'Feng' Gong (WH002) – 10.5"/27cm, 11"/28cm.

'Se' Gong (WH211) – Almost flat face but with a deep rim. 11"/28cm, 12.5"/32cm, 15"/38cm.

'Xiang Da' Gong (WH110) – 13"/33cm.

'Gou' Gong (WH010) – 16"/40cm.

'Jing Ban' Gong (WH005) – 8.5"/21.5cm.

'Che Sui' Gong (WH212) – 10"/25cm.

'Maxi' Gong (WH130)

4.5.6 Heng Luo Gong (WH012, WH233) *(tam-tam)*

These gongs are considered to give the most 'authentic' sounding, if those words can be used, of the Chinese gongs. Their outward appearance is similar to a Pasi Gong i.e. a small diameter flat centre with gently sloping face out to a reasonably deep rim (approaching 8cm on some larger versions). They are lathed on both faces and heavily hammered. The sound is a lovely deep, almost hollow crash with a long sustain and described by one dealer as 'industrial'. Available in diameters from 12"/30cm to 32"/81cm.

4.6   VIBRA

A trade name used by the Zanchi firm for cymbals and gongs sold to dealers in the USA and UK. See **UFIP** for further details.

4.7   SONA

SONA Gongs is a fairly recent addition to the world of gong making but have connections to one of the original exponents of using the gong for sound healing, Johannes Heimrath, who was cooperating with Paiste since the late seventies. From 1996 until 2004 the SONA gongs were produced as a special series exclusively for Heimrath at the Paiste workshop. Since 2006 they are manufactured in small numbers at a workshop on Heimrath's sound healing campus at Klein Jasedow in north east Germany, near to the Polish border. Thus the gongs share a heritage with Paiste, as originally they had been Sound Creation gongs modified according to Johannes Heimrath's specifications. Furthermore one of the gong makers at Klein Jasedow, Heiko Palkus, had once worked with Walter Meyer at Paiste. SONA also use blanks from a foundry in Germany used by Paiste as well as manufacturing the mallets both for Paiste and themselves. It's not surprising, therefore, that the gongs get compared with gongs made by their German neighbour.

There the similarity ends. The three models of gongs produced by SONA at the time of writing are intended for sound healing purposes, not music making in the first place (though there is nothing stopping them from being used for orchestral or band music). When the gongs are made, they are made with healing in mind and this is the focus of the manufacturing team. The three models are the 'Erde' (Earth) Gong, the 'Kosmos' (Cosmos) Gong and the "Mondin" (She-Moon) Gong.

The Erde Gongs have a very definite lineage to the Paiste Earth Sound Creation Gongs (models 3-3C) which at that time were influenced by Johannes Heimrath's therapeutic experience. It has a very heavily hammered face with definite raised hammer marks almost like bubbles on the metal face. They are made from a slightly thicker blank of nickel silver and available in two sizes:- 30"/75cm and 41"/105cm. They are described by SONA as having a 'mysterious multicoloured sound of a large, moving, dynamic flexible harmonic spectrum'.

The 'Kosmos' gong shares a lineage with the Paiste Symphonic Gong. Unlike the Paiste SG, the Kosmos Gong has a radially scraped face from the central disc and there are no characters or branding on the front of the gong. They are available in three sizes:- 30"/75cm, 41"/105cm and 60"/150cm. SONA describe them as having an embracing sound from a large full bandwidth with dynamic and powerful but balanced overtones. The standard size is the 105cm gong, and it differs from the Paiste Symphonic Gong as the sound is deeper, the whole instrument softer, thus readily supporting the more gentle playing techniques often applied in therapeutic situations.

The "Mondin" Gong is a completely new development, and its harmonic, long lasting sound (more than 2 minutes) doesn't change into 'crash mode' but keeps 'singing' even at higher dynamic levels. It was developed by Johannes Heimrath with the idea that it should not evoke any emotion connected to fear. This makes the She-Moon Gong very supportive for meditative therapeutic work. Its size is 30"/75cm.

In addition, SONA produce their own stands in a modular format that can be connected together in an aesthetically pleasing way – see next chapter.

SONA also make gongs for Tomek Czartoryski, a gong master from Poland and Don Conreaux, the 'Grand' gong master, considered by many to be the father of sound healing with gongs. Don and Tomek were instrumental in setting up a World Peace Garden near Krakow following the establishment of a similar garden by Don at Wimborne, Dorset in England. They began developing 'Maitreya' or 'Peace' Gongs for use by their students following their acquisition of gong blanks from one of the foundries used by Paiste. They first worked on a 24" version of the Maitreya gong which has its roots in the Paiste Symphonic Gong but it has a much deeper fundamental than an equivalent Symphonic or Planet Gong. The rim appears deeper and the face pressed out a bit more. It has radial scraping marks and the centre is decorated with either a Buddha's hand or a lotus flower. The Maitreya Gong is now available in 3 sizes:- 24"/60cm, 31"/75cm and 41"/105cm.

A recent development is the 'Reflection' Gong. Again it looks a bit like a Symphonic Gong but has a very polished centre section (hence 'reflection') and it speaks very easily. The sound is very similar to a 'Wind' gong or the Paiste Sound Creation Gong 'Fight/ Confrontation' and it seems ideal for smaller spaces or as a walking gong.

24" Maitreya Gong (courtesy Julian Marsden)

4.8   MEINL

Meinl are a German-based company that first started making cymbals from sheet metal back in 1953. At first they concentrated on making budget cymbals before expanding their range to higher quality cymbals for drummers and percussionists, as well as a wide range of other percussion instruments, especially Latin percussion instruments. Many of these are manufactured in the Far East and distributed from their German operation, though the cymbals are made in Germany.

Recently, Meinl introduced a range of gongs to its extensive catalogue of percussion instruments. The gongs were shown at the March 2011 Frankfurt Musikmesse and termed 'Symphonic Tam-Tams'. They are available in 4 sizes – 24"/60cm, 28"/70cm, 32"/80cm and 36"/90cm and a 40"/102cm diameter model is under development. The Meinl catalogue also gives a frequency range for the fundamental note – G2/G2# for the 24" model, E2 –F2 for the 28" model, C#2 – D2 for the 32" version and A#1 – B1 for the 36" model.

The gongs look very similar in appearance to Paiste Symphonic Gongs, which is not surprising, as the maker of these gongs is Broder Oetken, one time master gong maker at Paiste. They use blanks from one of the foundries that supplies gong blanks to Paiste. The visual differences are that the scrape marks are horizontal rather than vertical, have 'Symphonic Tam-Tam, Hand Crafted Masterpiece and made in Germany' printed onto the top face and the Meinl logo below it.

The gongs were very much prototypes made for the show so it will be interesting to see what becomes of this range over the coming years. I did get the chance to play some of the prototype and production models at Broder's workshop in September 2011 and I would describe the sound as equivalent to the Paiste Symphonic Gong but a slightly deeper tone size for size, which is in part due to a slightly thicker metal being used.

4.9   DREAM CYMBALS AND GONGS

Dream Cymbals and Gongs Inc. is a partnership of Canadian instrument designers and one of the oldest gong and cymbal making factories in

Meinl Symphonic Tam-tams (courtesy of Julian Marsden)

Close up of the Symphonic Tam-tam branding (courtesy of Julian Marsden)

Wuhan, China. They are exclusively made for Dream in this family owned factory. The 2011 range consisted of :

- Chao Gongs (6"/15cm to 60"/150cm)
- Feng (Wind) Gongs (6"/15cm to 60"/150cm)
- Jin Ban (chinese opera gong, 'bend up'), 7"/18cm to 9"/23cm)
- Tiger (chinese opera gong, 'bend down', 13"/33 cm to 16"/41cm)
- Bao gongs, available in either a machined or raw cast finish (4"/10cm to 40"/100cm in 1" steps).

They also offer a 'tuned' Bao Gong which has a lathed finish and a more focussed pitch and longer sustain than the standard Bao Gong. They are available in tunings from C2 – G5 either singly, in octave sets or custom designed sets.

4.10   OTHER MUSICAL INSTRUMENT MAKERS/ DISTRIBUTERS SELLING GONGS

A number of percussion and other musical instrument manufacturers and distributors offer gongs as part of their product line up. A few of these are detailed below:-

4.10.1 Percussion Plus

This firm does not make its own gongs and tam-tams but brands instruments from UFIP (a 28" Targo circular tam-tam) and Wuhan (several sizes of Chao gongs) with their own logo.

4.10.2 Stagg Music (EMD Music)

Stagg were established in 1995 and has its headquarters in Belgium. The firm provide a whole range of musical instruments and accessories from all over the world. They have an extensive range of cymbals and gongs sourced from China and re-branded with their own logo. The 2010 gong range ('T' range) consisted of:

2 'Mini' gongs – the 4.5"/11.5cm 'Moon' and 6.5"/16.5cm 'Stilt' gongs

4 sizes of 'Opera' gongs – 9"/22cm 'Hand', 11"/28cm 'Jing' and 'Wu' and 12"/30cm 'Su' gongs

4 sizes of 'Tiger' gongs – 12"/31cm, 13"/33cm and 14"/36 cm and the 14" 'Bass' gong.

These are all of a similar appearance – flat centre, gently sloping away mid to edge section with a turned over rim. The rest of the range consists of 8 'Wind' Gongs – 16"/40cm to 36"/90cm and 14 'Tam-tam' gongs (Chao gongs) from 15"/38 cm to 40"/100 cm.

4.11   SPECIALIST GONG MAKERS

In addition to the main gong makers, there are a number of individuals who are making their own gongs and selling them, often to individuals, but some going to larger percussion instrument makers. Some of these individuals are retired master gong makers from Paiste but the lure of gong making and experimenting with new gong designs means that they continue to work in this fascinating field.

4.11.1 Steve Hubback

Steve Hubback is a Welsh-born musician, bronzesmith and metal sculptor who spends much of his time in Prague in the Czech Republic and in Scandinavia. He left Wales for Paris in 1981 and started to experiment with very small drumsets and more unusual percussion. During this time he was influenced by the music of Andrea Centazzo (as well as many

Steve Hubback Astrology Gong
(courtesy of Steve Hubback)

others including Terje Rypdal and Tony Oxley) who was one of the very few improvisers playing gongs and metal percussion.

Steve made his first gong in Aarhus Denmark in 1990 and, although rough, it had interesting qualities. This inspired him to explore working with metal to make instruments and sculptures, He learnt welding from a metal working friend and a Norwegian blacksmith who after years of observation, eventually gave Steve a demonstration of master forge craft, a magical experience which has stayed with him ever since. In 1992 he hammered out what was at the time the Worlds biggest gong which was 2.5 metres in diameter and made from 4mm thick 304 stainless steel, weighing 155 kg. It took a month of continuous work to create it.

In the early 1990's he had a vivid dream where a percussionist was playing a number of otherwordly percussion instruments on a very unique drumset that had a large living bronze dragon's wing instead of a ride cymbal. This image stayed in Steve's mind and after much work it was translated and forged into the Dragon cymbal.

Steve Hubback Dragon Gong
(courtesy of Steve Hubback)

Since then Steve has invented and pioneered many cymbal, gong and percussion sculptures. He has developed special techniques for his work and most of his creations are made from bronze. Some works are in stainless steel especially those for outdoor installation and a small amount of work in nickel silver.

His sculptures have been exhibited in many countries from Iceland to the Czech Republic and include unusual places such as a Welsh forest in which Steve created a garden of sound sculptures in Stainless Steel. In 2006, Paiste sponsored Steve with some of their patented sound alloy. A selection of gong sculptures were created and exhibited in London and in the Netherlands. A performance of the London exhibition was recorded and is now available from FMR-Records. Steve Hubback London Vaults FMRCD235-0707.

He continues to invent and create unique gong and percussion sculptures. His creations are played by some of the world's best percussionists including Paolo Vinaccia, Paul Clarvis, Evelyn Glennie, Andrea Centazzo, Snorre Bjerck, Birgit Lokke, Marilyn Mazur

Steve Hubback OM Gong
(courtesy of Steve Hubback)

and Chris Whitten amongst others as well as many shamanic healers, sound healers, occultists and those influenced by gong energies. Steve is heavily influenced by dreams and shapes in nature. He makes his own sticks, mallets and parts of his percussion set are made from wood from European forests.

4.11.2 Matt Nolan

Matt Nolan is a cymbal and gong maker working in the ancient city of Bath in the south-west of England. Matt is an electronics engineer by training but was also a drummer and percussionist in his spare time. Over time, the pull of working with his hands on creative metal sounds as well as a desire to create new and interesting sounds and shapes for

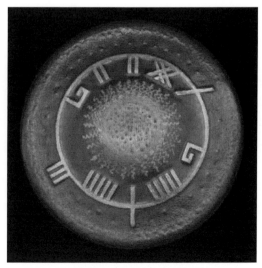

Matt Nolan Ogham Gong
(courtesy of Matt Nolan)

cymbals and then for gongs, got the better of him. Today he makes a range of cymbals for the kit drummer (especially the jazz drummer) using different metals and decoration, including interesting hammering marks, colours, shapes and designs. He began by teaching himself in the mid 2000s but meeting and talking to people like Steve Hubback around this time allowed Matt to try different techniques, which helped expand the range of instruments being made. Matt describes his works as 'artisan metal percussion instruments'. He draws on inspiration from the natural world, geometric shapes and symbolism from ancient civilisations.

Matt Nolan Bat Wing Gong
(courtesy of Matt Nolan)

Matt now produces a range of gongs and musical sculptures to complement his cymbals. These are made from a variety of metals and include bronze (especially phosphor bronze), nickel silver and stainless steel. The gongs are essentially 'wind gongs' in appearance though he has experimented with bossed gongs and some gongs with a small turned over rim. The gongs themselves are highly individual and possess many sounds and tonal colours. Several nickel silver ones demonstrated to me on a visit to his workshop had large crashing overtones and shimmer but with a strong fundamental for 22" and 24" gongs. They had particularly unique hammer patterns on a whitish metal face with purple and blue hues around the central face. One had a particularly good howling screech mixed in with the overtones. The phosphor bronze gong had a darker, tuned fundamental but supported with warm overtones and a colour not far from certain German-made gongs. They all respond well to flumi and in particular to bowing with a violin bow. Gong diameters tend to be in the 20"/50cm – 24"/60cm range, but both smaller and larger gongs are occasionally produced.

The sound sculptures are varied and include a large 'bat's wing' and an impressive 'Hand'. This latter instrument is made from sheet bronze in the form of a one metre long human left or right hand and is available in two weights. For an additional fee, this gong could be made to represent your own hand! Matt will also make bespoke gongs for customers, incorporating designs and logos specified by the customer into the gong. He is also developing other percussion instruments such as triangles and bells and is making hand cymbals for

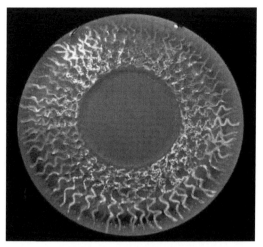

Matt Nolan Solsbury Gong
(courtesy of Matt Nolan)

orchestral use. Matt's customers have included Dame Evelyn Glennie, Björk, Danny Elfman, The Boston Symphony Orchestra, The Finnish National Opera, The Bergen Philharmonic, The Royal Opera House Covent Garden, The Illinois Symphony Orchestra, Massive Attack and Lea Mullen (percussionist with Happy Mondays and George Michael).

4.11.3 Walter Mayer – Creative Gong Sounds

When it comes to the world of Western gongs, there is one person that has had more influence than any other on the sounds, tonal colours and visual impact of German gongs. That person is Walter Meyer. Walter spent over 30 years working for Paiste beginning as an electrician and finally becoming a master gong maker. He was responsible for developing the Sound Creation Gong and the Tuned Gong ranges as well as influencing the other gong ranges made by Paiste. The 80"/200cm Symphonic Gong at Paiste was Walter's creation, as is the 60"/150cm Symphonic Gong currently owned by the Sound Healer Sheila Whittaker which Walter considers to be the best gong in the world! The Sound Creation Gong range resulted from a desire to experiment with new and unusual gong sounds, and the Tuned Gongs were made in response to requests from percussionists and composers to develop a gong that had more sustain

Walter Mayer 'White Tai Loi' Gong
(courtesy of Pauline McCrann)

and volume than the Balinese gamelan gongs.

Although no longer working for Paiste, Walter is still very much involved with gong making at his home near Rendsburg in north-east Germany. He has been making one off special gongs for various people over the years including Aiden McIntyre, Don Conreaux and Sheila Whittaker and training or working with other gong makers such as Broder Oetken and with Johannes Heimrath and SONA gongs. At the time of writing, Walter was currently working on re-introducing the Sound Creation Gong No.4 'Water' in different thickness of metal and aims to follow this by SCG No. 1 'Sun'. Walter is also happy to make gongs for anyone, for a price!

Two master gong makers par excellence – Broder Oetken (l) and Walter Meyer(r) next to an Oetken 'Sol' gong

4.11.4 Broder Oetken

Broder Oetken was a master gong maker at Paiste, working alongside Walter Meyer for many years. He eventually left Paiste after that company wanted to concentrate on its Symphonic and Planet gong ranges whereas Broder wanted to carry on with developing new gong sounds in the tradition of the Sound Creation series.

Recently he has set up his own gong making company – Oetken Gongs, not too far from Paiste in Osterrönfeld near Rendsburg in northeast Germany. With access to the foundries supplying blanks for Paiste, he has been commissioned to produce a range of tam-tams for the Meinl Company. These 'Symphonic Tam-Tams' were first displayed at the Frankfurt Musikmesse in 2011. They are produced in the same manner as the Paiste Symphonic Gong, though Broder experimented with different thicknesses of metal. For instance, the 28"/66cm Meinl Symphonic tam-tam started out as a 2.0 mm thick prototype but the production versions are 1.4mm.

Broder is also looking to develop his own range of gongs in between the commissions for Meinl. His first bespoke gongs were a pair of 'Sol'

Broder Oetken's workshop with several Meinl tam-tams waiting final tuning.

or Sun gongs made at my suggestion and tuned to B1 but 36"/91cm in diameter with radial scrape marks. I have also suggested other gongs such as 'Terra' and 'Lunar' plus a range of Zodiac sign gongs with tunings based on the Ruling Planet for the astrological sign in question. It will be interesting to watch his work develop over the coming years.

4.11.5 Michael Paiste

Michael Paiste began working at the Paiste cymbal factory in Notwill in 1986 mainly involved with the development of cymbals. He left after 12 years as he wanted to specialise in custom made cymbals but this was not in line with company policy at the time. For the past 13 years he has developed a range of visually and aurally stunning cymbals and gongs from a variety of metals. His gong range includes a 14"/35cm bronze Volcano Gong, a 30"/76cm brass Volcano Gong, a 24"/61cm Water gong, a 24"/61cm Heavy Wind Gong, a 40"/102cm Wind Gong and the evocatively named 24"/61cm 'Screaming' Gong. His gongs are made to order and pictures can be found on his 'MySpace' page.

REFERENCES – CHAPTER 4

1. Cousto, Hans: *The Cosmic Octave: Origin of Harmony, Planets, Tones, Colour : the power of inherent vibrations* Life Rhythm, 1988, CA, USA

2. Conreaux, Don: *Gongs of our Solar System: Tonal Guide for Healing through Sound* Mysterious Tremendum, 2002, New York

3. Heimrath, Johannes: *The Healing Power of the Gong.* MMB Music Inc. 1994, St Louis, USA

5. GONGS FROM SOUTH-EAST ASIA

5.1   INTRODUCTION

No book on gongs would be complete without discussing gongs from South-East Asia, particularly Burma, Vietnam and Indonesia. This part of the world is famed for the tuned or bossed gong, the most famous of which, arguably, are the gongs belonging to the Indonesian gamelan orchestra. It is often thought that the largest gongs produced in this region are about 39"/100cm in diameter but they can be much larger, sometimes approaching 80"/200cm in diameter.

Whilst researching this book, it dawned on me that the wide variety of gongs from this area could warrant a book in its own right. In this book, I can only scratch the surface and have concentrated on gongs from the three aforementioned countries. During my research, however, I unearthed such a book, or rather a learned paper, which was published in 1939.

Gong und Gongspeil (Gongs and Gong Play)[1] was written by Heinrich Simbringer and published in the *International Archive for Ethnography*. It is a work that looks at gongs and gong making right across South-East Asia as well as the Philippines, Japan, Annam (part of modern Vietnam) and Formosa (now Taiwan). Sadly (for me at least) the work is published in German and I am not aware of an English translation, but a skim through its nearly 200 pages hints at an astonishing work and provides a unique reference. Perhaps someone someday will translate it.

The music and instruments of this region have been studied on several occasions throughout the 20th century, mainly by Dutch and German ethnomusicologists. Indonesia and Java have been the focus for a couple of notable works published about gong making. Edward Jacobson and

J.H. van Hasselt studied gong making in Semarang in 1907[2] and this was followed by two famous studies of gong making in different parts of Java by Jaap Kunst in 1933 and 1949, published in his work *Music in Java*[3]. Both studies looked at gong making throughout Java, but particularly in Semarang and compared how things had changed since the 1907 study. Kunst was particularly concerned with the negative effects on the industry around the time of the Second World War due to shortages of tin and copper. Fortunately, an interest in the gamelan from musicologists and composers from the West, particularly the USA, saw a resurgence from the early 1960s.

5.2   GAMELAN GONGS

A gamelan is a musical ensemble from Indonesia, primarily associated with the islands of Bali and Java though variations can be found throughout the Malay Archipelago. The word 'gamelan' is derived from the word 'gamel' which most commonly translates as 'to hit with a hammer'. Adding '-an' to the word converts it from a verb to a noun. Hammers are not normally used to play the instruments but are used in the making of some of them. Gamelan really refers to a collection of instruments – gongs, metallophones, drums, stringed instruments and occasionally voices. Each instrument is tuned together as an ensemble which means that instruments are not normally interchangeable between orchestras.

There are several tunings that the gamelans use, the two most common being slendro and pelog. Slendro has five notes per 'octave' with equally spaced intervals whereas pelog has seven notes per 'octave' with unequal intervals. Again, the actual individual notes may differ between gamelans which is why they are constructed as a single entity, the tunings of each instrument being complimentary to each other. Many gamelans now exist in the West, either as part of a university or music college or as part of some community group. This is similar in many ways to the number of samba bands being established outside of their native Brazil. Several dozen exist in the UK – see www.gamelan.org.uk

Much has been written about the gamelan[4,5,6] so this book will just concentrate on the gongs, mainly those of the Javanese and Balinese gamelan. The gongs of a Gamelan tend to fall into two categories;- those that are suspended vertically and those that are supported horizontally on a rack or on the knees or a cushion.

5.2.1 Vertically Suspended Gongs

The vertically suspended gongs are the largest in the gamelan. They are used to begin, end and punctuate different segments of the metric cycle. There are differences between Javanese and Balinese hanging gongs but all are sub-divided into three types – Bass Voice, Middle Voice and Treble Voice.

Bass Voice

The bass voice gongs in Java consist of two types. The *Gong Ageng* is the largest and deepest of the gongs, often 40"/100cm in diameter. There is usually at least one Gong Ageng, sometimes two, depending on how many scales are used in the gamelan. This gong begins and ends the metric cycle. The other bass voice gong is the *Gong Suwouk*. This is smaller than the Ageng and there are usually two per scale and it is used to begin and end metric sub cycles.

The bass voice gongs in Bali consist of the *Gong Wadon* and the *Gong Lanang*. The Gong Wadon is the largest Balinese gong at about 38"/95cm diameter. It has a thinner face than the Lanang which means it vibrates more freely. The Lanang is smaller, slightly higher in pitch and has a thicker face. Both are used to begin and end the metric cycle.

All these gongs have a beautiful deep bell-like boom and are rarely played *forte*, though the sustain is relatively short lived.

Middle Voice

The Javanese middle voice gong is the *Kempul*. These are 15"/40cm to 20"/50cm in diameter, with one or more per scale. They punctuate half way to the mid point of the cycle. In Bali, the middle voice gongs are the *Kempur*, a gong 16"/42cm to 25"/62cm in diameter, punctuating the mid point of the cycle, and the *Bheri*, a gong with a recessed boss. In smaller ensembles, a Kempur can take the place of a Wadon. All these gongs have a very clean, mid bell-like tone.

Treble Voice

The treble voice gongs consist of the *Kemong* in both Bali and Java, which is high in pitch, and the *Klintong* which is only used in Bali. This latter gong is played with a wooden beater producing a piercing sound. All other gongs in this section are played with a padded mallet or occasionally as with the bass gongs, with the fleshy part of the fist.

Gong Ageng and Gong Suwouk

5.2.2 Horizontal Gongs

The horizontal gongs are played either in racks, singularly supported on a box resonator, or in the lap. The Javanese version is the *Bonang*, a double horizontal row of 10 to 14 gongs with round bosses. Other types are the *Bonang Panerus*, an octave higher than the standard Bonang and the *Bonang Panembung*, which is an octave lower. Finally there is the *Kenong*, a large deep-rimmed gong suspended on a cord over a box resonator and used for dividing the musical cycle.

Gong Bonang

Gong Kenong

The Balinese versions are the *Trompong,* consisting of 12 gongs with conical bosses, played by one person and the *Reong,* a horizontal row of small gongs with conical bosses played by one or more players. The gongs in both countries are played with cord wound wooden sticks.

Both countries have several small hand held gongs, or ones that are supported on the lap or a resonator box. They are used in various parts of the cycle, often with cord wound beaters.

The gongs of the gamelan are very distinctive, with a pronounced boss which can be either round or conical, a wide face and a deep rim sloping back towards the centre line of the gong. They are usually made from bronze though iron is not uncommon, and are made in a smithy known as a *besalen.*

5.2.3 How The Gongs Are Made

A significant number of people are required to make the gong. There is the master gong maker and his assistant, one or two people on the bellows for the furnace, plus several people for the hammering process. In addition, several helpers are needed to move the gong around, make up the clay anvil supports etc. A large Ageng Gong can take two to three days to make. The method described below is typical not just of Indonesia and the gamelan gongs, but of gong making in this part of South-East Asia as a whole.

In order to make the gongs, the bronze must first be prepared. The mixture normally consists of 10 parts copper to 3 parts tin, melted together in a clay crucible in a charcoal fire powered by hand operated bellows. The molten metal is checked for consistency by pouring out two coin-sized discs of bronze into a mould in the earth floor. One is broken in two to check the grain size and one is hammered until it is 2 mm thick to check malleability. Extra copper or tin can be added depending on the results of these tests.

Once the metal mixture is of the correct consistency the metal is poured into a pre-heated concave mould in the earth floor. Once solidified, the disc is re-heated to red hot by the master gong maker before it is hammered using steel hammers with long heads, almost as long as the handles and weighing up to 9kg! The hammering is done in 15 to 30 second bouts by up to four men in a co-ordinated fashion before the disc has to be returned to the fire. During the hammering the disc is rotated by the gong maker. The anvils used are predominantly stone, though metal versions exist. Between hammering, the chief assistant remoulds clay mounds around the anvil to support the ever growing disc.

Once the basic face reaches the required diameter, the inward sloping edge is formed by hammering on the anvil which now has a steep sloping mound of clay to support the gong in this unusual position. Once the edge is formed, the boss of the gong is formed by gently hammering out the centre of the gong into a depression in the floor. Attention then turns back to the rim/side which is hammered against a vertical stone anvil. Finally, a steel hoop is placed around the base of the gong to prevent deformation, then the gong is reheated and quickly quenched in cold water.

Once cool, the gong is cold hammered to give its final shape and tuning using small hammers. One aspect of this process is the forming of the gently sloping 'shoulder' between the flat central area surrounding the boss, and the edge of the top face of the gong. This shoulder (known as a 'Recap') is formed by clamping the gong to a horizontal anvil by the use of a downward facing wooden stake at the end of a 5-metre-long-lever. Whilst the flat central section is held in place, the side of the gong next to the stake is hammered until the curvature is fixed. Final tuning is achieved using clay pieces on different parts of the metal and hammering against wooden formers. Most of the tuning is done by hammering, though some filing is still used.

Normally the black oxide layer is completely removed using files and emery cloth, leaving a bright shiny gold finish on the outside, but the oxide layer is left on the inside. Occasionally, the oxide layer is left over the entire gong except for the boss, which can then be highly polished.

In most cases, a complete gamelan can be obtained from a manufacturer but an internet search shows that it is possible to buy individual elements of a gamelan (including the gongs), from a dealer in Bali.

The sound of a gamelan is quite unlike any other orchestra or ensemble and is difficult to describe in words so I would encourage listening to one if the opportunity arises. The gongs themselves fall into two distinct sound areas. The larger Agong, Kempuls and other hanging gongs have a sort of 'duum' resonating sound with a different pitch depending on the size of the gong. The sustain is short lived. The horizontal gongs like the Bonang have a clearer bell like sound, quite metallic due to the use of cord wound beaters but again, the sustain is very short lived. This is to allow faster rhythms to be played on these gongs, without build up of overtones. Neither type of gong is played loudly, especially the hanging gongs, which rarely get above *mezzo forte*.

5.3 VIETNAMESE GONGS

As in other parts of South-East Asia, particularly Burma, Thailand and Cambodia, the gong plays an important part in Vietnamese ceremonies, rites and religions. They are believed to be inhabited by spirits and represent a form of communication between humans and the spirit world. A person who possesses many gongs is highly respected, not because of wealth but because they are protected by many spirits. All Vietnamese families own or have access to gongs and they are often used during significant feasts, festivals, the birth of a child (I played a 'Moon' gong after the birth of our son – Moon being the ruling planet for his astrological sign of Cancer), the death of a family member, weddings, and even repairs to the house! Often, several people in the village will gather together with a variety of gongs, as an ensemble, with gongs ranging from 10"/25cm to 31"/80cm in diameter.

The Vietnamese gong shares a general shape with other gongs in this region. The boss is set in a flat face, which is heavily hammer-marked. Between the flat face and the rim, there is a shallow 'channel'. The rim turns over and is either perpendicular to the face or gently slopes back in on itself. The rim is not very deep, usually between 1cm to 5cm depending on the size of the gong. The gongs are normally made from bronze though iron and brass versions are common. The hammer marks are normally round and small and don't cut into the instrument like

Small Taiwanese gong

other Far Eastern gongs. The surface finish is a brown oxide layer which readily helps distinguish them from the neighbouring Burmese/Thai gongs which are dark green or black in colour. Their tone is bright and bell-like for the smaller gongs, moving to a richer 'duum' tone for the larger gongs. There is a reasonable sustain, but not prolonged. Again, the best tone is obtained when played *piano* to *mezzo forte*. Anything louder tends to jar, with a sharp 'donk' sound and the sustain immediately returns to that associated with more gentle playing.

5.4 BURMESE/THAI GONGS

Gongs from Burma (or Myanmar as it is now known) have a long history and are often quoted as being the beginnings of gong making in South-East Asia along with China, Java and Amman. The Burmese gong has influenced other gong types in this region and is very similar to those found in Thailand, so they are often grouped together. Although there are several types of Burmese gong, the most common are the temple gongs and the triangular-shaped Kyeezee or 'spinning' gong.

The shape of the Burmese gong is one of the most recognisable. They are normally made from bronze and have a prominent round boss sitting on a slightly convex curving face with the edge of the boss being slightly recessed. There is a prominent lip moving over to a gently inwardly sloping rim which is deep – usually 1.5"/3cm to 5"/12cm depending on the size of the gong. The oxidised layer is left on the metal and can either be slate grey, black or bottle green in colour. The oxidised layer is often scraped to reveal various patterns, with lotus flower petals or star flower mandala patterns being the most common.

The actual construction of the gong is very similar to the method described for gamelan gongs (see Section 5.2.3). There are some detailed differences – the rim, for instance, doesn't need as much clay to support it and the hammers used are a little smaller. Some images I have seen show small blemishes, cracks and holes being filled in with a type of weld, but overall the lineage between these gongs and other gongs in this part of the world can be seen in their construction.

Over the past fifteen years or so, Burmese gongs have become much more widely available in the West. This is partly due to the withdrawal of the tuned gongs made by Paiste and the affordability of the Burmese gong. Both Kolberg Percussion and the German 'Gong Factory.com' website supply individual gongs from 6"/15cm to 36"/90cm diameter as well as chromatic sets of 13 gongs, tuned C2 to C6 (nominally A4 = 443 Hz) over four octaves. They also provide the tuned gongs needed for the operas *Turando'* and *Madame Butterfly*. Originally, these gongs were supplied by

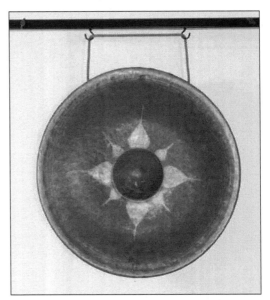

Burmese / Thai gong

one of the families forming part of the UFIP union and most Italian opera companies stick with specially commissioned gongs from UFIP. Other opera companies are now using the Burmese option. Other suppliers offer small Burmese gongs but the prices do vary considerably so do a bit of checking around before purchasing. It is worth searching for them in antique and junk shops as many Burmese gongs were used as 'dinner' gongs in hotels and guest houses or just as ornaments. The 22" Burmese gong in my collection cost £15 from an antiques shop in Salisbury, England – a bargain when a new one costs several hundred pounds!

Burmese Kyeezee

One thing to bear in mind when playing these gongs is that they need to be played with padded beaters and played quietly. They are cast gongs and can crack if played with a hard beater or struck with any force. The sound of the gong is a lovely low 'dong' with little overtones and no splash. The decay is fairly short lived and lasts the same length of time whether struck *forte* or *piano*.

The 'Kyeezee' is a triangular-shaped piece of bronze or brass, often decorated and carved and quite thick in cross-section. It is suspended on a cord at its mid point. When it is struck, it has a piercing bell-like tone and spinning the Kyeezee gives a warbling effect. They are often used in meditation. Both Zildjian and UFIP make their own versions of the Kyeezee called 'Burmese Bells'.

5.5   WELDED GONGS

Several years ago I discovered some Burmese-looking gongs in a New Age shop. They were painted a gold colour and, on closer inspection I discovered that they had been made by welding (!) the boss to four sections which formed the face, and then the face was welded to the rim. I didn't get the chance to hear the tonal qualities. Whilst researching this book I also found a tourist site offering trips to a gong smithy in Malaysia. The photographs of the smithy showed piles of gong faces and rims waiting to be welded together! This is not generally considered to be the preferred way to make gongs so will not be covered any further.

REFERENCES – CHAPTER 5

1. Simbringer, Heinrich, *Gong und Gongspeil, International Archive for Ethnography*, part 36, E.J Brill, Leiden, Holland, 1939.

2. Jacobson, E & van Hasselt J.H., *De Gong – Fabricatie te Semarang.* EJ Brill, Leidon, 1907. Translated into English by Toth, Andrew, *The Manufacture of Gongs in Semarang*, Indonesia 19, April 1975.

3. Kunst, J, *Music in Java*, M. Nijhoff, 1973

4. Balibeyond.com – Gamelan Instruments Document

5. *Gong Smithing in Twentieth Century Surakarta, Asian Art and Culture*, Vol.VIII, No.3, (Fall 1995), Oxford University Press.

6. Sorrell, N *A Guide to Gamelan*, Faber and Faber, 1990, London

6. STANDS, BEATERS AND BAGS

This section will look at some of the items needed to support the gong, make sounds from it and protect it.

6.1 STANDS

Unless you intend to support your gong by hand all the time then you will need some form of support for it. When considering the purchase or construction of a stand there are a few pre-requisites that need to be considered.

Support – The stand should be able to support the weight of the gong and the forces created whilst it is swinging around without deforming or cracking. This is particularly essential for the larger gongs (especially large Chao gongs) due to their heavy weight.

Stability – There is nothing worse than a gong stand falling over, especially during a concert or sound healing session. When played, a gong can swing backwards and forwards or side to side causing the stand to rock. If the gong's centre of gravity passes a certain point, the gong and stand will topple over. The British 'gallows' stand and the Paiste and Chinese floor stands can be susceptible to this as these stands have high centres of gravity but small feet.

Portability – Stands can be quite large so their ability to be dismantled into easily carried parts is desirable. Square stands can usually be completely dismantled whereas the circular types are more bulky. Trying to get a large circular stand into the back of a small European hatchback type car could be an interesting challenge!

Affordability – Most percussionists and sound healers are prepared to pay a lot of money for good quality gongs but are somewhat reluctant to pay large sums of money for stands. After all, that money can be put towards purchasing more gongs! In many cases, good quality stands can range in price from £150/$200 to £300/$400. It has to be said, however, that a good quality stand is worth its weight in gold. Still, many people look for innovative alternatives or make their own. My first stand (a square stand capable of supporting a 40" gong – see page 57) was built for me by a man with his own metal workshop in his garage. It cost the princely sum of £30 and it is still doing sterling service 25 years later! By all means, consider making your own or adapting something suitable, but consider the other three pre-requisites above.

There are basically three types of gong stand for vertically supported gongs:-

square/rectangular

round/circular and the

uniquely British 'gallows' stand.

6.1.1 Square Stands

Square stands are the most popular of gong stands, being simple to construct, assemble and dismantle. They are normally made from tubular or square section steel and can be painted, powder-coated or polished. Some are made from aluminium and some from stainless steel. Normally, two hooks are fixed in the top horizontal bar from which to hang the gong from, though additional hooks may be added to other parts of the stand for beaters. Square stands can also be height adjustable by using telescopic legs, where the vertical uprights slide inside the tubing of the outer frame. Those with enough height adjustment can allow a second gong to be hung from the bottom horizontal bar. The locking of these uprights is usually achieved by the use of wing bolts, sometimes just gripping the inner tube by friction (e.g. Paiste Square Stand) or into pre-drilled holes in the inner tube (e.g. Matthew Beavis Custom Gong Stands). Occasionally, the stands are fitted with castors to enable the stands to be moved around with relative ease.

In all cases, nuts, bolts and other fixings should be checked for tightness after assembly both to avoid a potential collapse and, just as important, to avoid annoying rattles from the stand whilst playing the gong. Additionally, for height adjustable stands, wrapping insulation or a similar type of sticky tape around the inner tubes is sometimes required to ensure a tighter fit into the outer tube, and prevent rattling. For the Paiste adjustable height square gong stands, it is also a good idea to check the horizontal alignment with a spirit level.

Paiste large square stand with 36″ Symphonic Gong

Square stands are made by Paiste, Sabian, Zildjian, UFIP, Stagg, Yamaha, Percussion Plus and Matthew Beavis to name a few. Most square stands are available in at least two sizes – small (for gongs up to 30″/76cm) and large (for gongs from 32″/81cm up to 40″/102cm) though some do a variety of sizes. The Paiste range consists of 'Square' (sometimes termed Square Orchestral) in seven sizes, 'Set – Square' (holds two gongs) in five sizes, and they used to produce 'Set-Rectangular' for three or more gongs such as an octave's worth of tuned gongs or several Sound Creation Gongs. There was also a 'Vertical Rectangle' for the three Sound Creation Chakra gongs. These rectangular stands are not offered in their current catalogue. Paiste use a heavy duty square section tubular steel painted in a black lacquer.

The 'Custom Gong Stands' made by Matthew Beavis in the UK (Kent) are lovely pieces of engineering. Again, square section tubing is used, but the cross sections are narrower than Paiste. The wing bolts locate into holes drilled into the inner sections giving an easy assembly but are restricted to about five pre-set heights. The steel has a powder-coated finish. Two sizes are available – medium and large, though a small stand is available for 22" and 24" gongs on special order. (See photos on page 7 and 41 for examples of Custom Gong Stands).

6.1.2 Round Stands

Round, arched and 'C'-shaped stands are also available for gongs, though only a few manufacturers offer them. This is partly due to the relative difficulty of dismantling the stands. The 'hoop' tends to be a one-piece construction of wrought iron or tubular steel making the larger versions difficult to carry or stow in a car. The feet or legs, however, can be removed for transport.

The main advantage of round stands is aesthetic. The circumference of the stand compliments the circular form of the gong bringing a certain balance to the whole ensemble. This is one of the reasons that they tend to be favoured by sound healers and yoga leaders.

The most common round stands are those made by Paiste. Two models are currently available – 'Orchestral Round' and 'Floor'.

The Orchestral Round stand comprises a tubular steel hoop painted black with two lugs on the bottom half which slot into a pair of V-shaped legs. The diameter of the hoop reflects the diameter of the gong that can be hung from it. Paiste currently offers six different sizes of stand, with stands for the 60"/150cm and 80"/205cm Symphonic Gongs made to order. The name 'Orchestral' is a misnomer – Paiste don't currently advertise it as such in their catalogue but distributers often describe it this way in their lists. I have never seen this stand used by either professional or amateur orchestras, and a straw poll of some percussion colleagues has revealed that these stands have only been spotted where multiple gongs and tam-tams have been required. The main reason that this style of stand is not used is that orchestral tam-tams are played by standing over the instrument – the top of the stand coming up to waist or chest height. This allows greater control of the instrument, especially for damping it which is usually performed by pressing the hand on the back face of the tam-tam, forcing it against the leg. The round stand does not allow this. Also, the legs take up a lot of floor space and present a tripping hazard. As any percussionist will tell you, space is often at a premium in the percussion section especially in some concert venues, so compact stands are favoured.

One musical genre where the round stand is particularly favoured is heavy rock where the gong on its stand forms an imposing back drop to a drum kit set up. (see video footage for Queen, Led Zeppelin and The Who, amongst others). They have also found favour with brass bands again because of the imposing backdrop and symmetrical form given to the band layout.

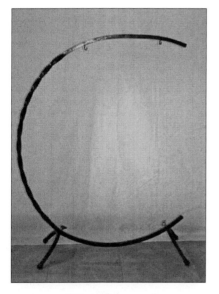

Paiste Floor stand

Paiste Round Orchestral stand

The Paiste floor stand is made from twisted wrought iron in the form of a letter 'C' with two small feet at right angles to the hoop. The feet are normally fixed by wing nuts. It is popular due to its elegance, compact height and ease of assembly. They are available in 10 sizes to accommodate gongs from 20"/51cm to 38"/91cm. A number of orchestras use this form of stand due to its small footprint and ability of the player to lean over the gong. Sound healers and yoga leaders also use this stand as they can play the gong sitting down. The stand's drawback is that a swinging gong can make the stand very unstable and the wing nuts can slacken off during playing. There are also Chinese round 'floor' stands which are made from tubular steel or aluminium.

6.1.3   'Gallows' Stand

This type of stand was developed for orchestral use, being light, portable and compact. They take up the minimum of space, but give all round accessibility for playing and damping purposes. They are used extensively by British orchestras using Paiste tam-tams and gongs.

The stand normally comprises a single upright strut with a V- or a T-shaped head from which the gong is hung. The bottom of the strut is fixed to a pair of legs in a V-shaped form (the strut attached to the point of the 'V' with swivel bolts) or a H-shaped foot with the strut attached to a spigot on the cross bar of the 'H'. They are normally made from square section steel and the height can be adjusted to support different sized gongs. JAM Percussion in Liverpool makes a version where the legs fold back on themselves, making the stand very portable. I use this regularly for orchestral concerts because of this portability. The JAM Percussion stand will take a Paiste tam-tam up to about 38"/91cm in diameter. Chalklin Percussion also makes a version with the H- shaped foot which is detachable for transport. Several individuals have also made their own versions of these stands.

JAM Percussion gallows stand with Paiste Planet Gong 'Mars'

JAM Percussion gallows stand – folded

The main disadvantage of the gallows stand is its inherent instability. Any significant swinging of the gong can lead to it toppling over as the centre of gravity is quite high with little lateral stability. The stand can be stabilised by placing a hand on top of the stand. However, the sound therapy techniques of 'Swinging Door' and 'Gong with the Wind' (see Chapter 8 on playing techniques) makes this stand unsuitable for this type of playing.

During the writing of this book, Meinl introduced their own take on the gallows stand at the 2011 Frankfurt Musikmesse. It has an adjustable vertical square section steel post surmounted by a T-shaped head. It also has another bracket part way up the post to support what Meinl call a 'dampening disc' which can be angled to touch the back of the gong and damp some of the sound. The foot is a large squared off C-shape, but is wider than the Chalklin equivalent and comes with an optional four castor wheels and appears to be more inherently stable than the other gallows stand described here.

6.1.4 Boom Cymbal Stand

For drummers and percussionists, a boom cymbal stand (a stand where the cymbal is attached to a rod that passes through a variable angle mount on to the tripod stand) can make an effective temporary stand for a small gong. There are, however, stability problems if the boom is extended too far from the main stand and a risk of the bottom of the gong striking the upright if the boom is not extended far enough!

6.1.5 Wooden Stands

Wooden stands have been used for centuries to support gongs, especially in South East Asia. In the West, there is a preference for metal stands especially where flexibility for mounting different sized gongs is required plus repeated assembly and dismantling, where wood often exhibits excessive wear. Wood also needs to be strong to support the weight of the gong and the forces encountered when it swings. Hence wooden stands tend to be made from hardwoods which are getting more difficult to source due to conservation and sustainability issues. In the UK, very few distributers offer wooden stands and where they are offered, the costs are on a par with the more expensive types of square stands. In the USA, there is a wide choice of wooden stands from Gongs Unlimited, and if portability is not an issue, they make great stands as well as fine items of furniture in their own right.

Wood does lend itself to being carved and decorated and hence becomes something more than just a support for the gong. Gamelan stands are beautifully turned and shaped hardwoods, and many temple gongs are hung from large baulks of timber, heavily carved and beautifully painted or gilded.

6.1.6 Drum Racks

Drum racks are a familiar piece of hardware for drummers of rock groups who have a drum kit outside of the 'norm' and don't want the hassle of setting up many individual stands for their drums, tom-toms and cymbals. Drum racks are essentially various lengths of tubular steel (normally stainless) held together by metal or plastic corner pieces secured by long wing bolts. Various accessories can be attached to the steel tubes such as cymbal heads, hooks, tubular steel arms for supporting 'effects etc'. The racks are modular so you can add pieces as required. They have the appearance of scaffolding but are much more refined than that.

One of the most well-known makers of drum racks is Gibraltar. They make drum racks and accessories from 1.5"/3.5cm diameter stainless steel and are widely available and reasonably priced. The gong player Michael Bettine uses them and there are some good pictures of his gong set ups on his website www.gongtopia.com.

Similar to a drum rack is the gong rack made by SONA in Germany (www.sonasounds.com). This is a cross between a round gong stand and a square gong stand that can also be added to as required. The basic stand comprises uprights, a semi circular top piece which is available in various diameters (65cm – 120cm) to accommodate different gong sizes. There are also telescopic cross-braces. Various joint pieces that can be used to add further top and brace sections to extend the stand. The basic 'kit' consists of uprights, feet, horizontal bar and a semi-circular top piece for a 75cm gong. Feet with castors can also be purchased. These stands are particularly pleasing on the eye as the hoop compliments the circular form of the gong, and it has the flexibility to be extended as required

6.1.7 Home Made

Anyone with a modicum of engineering skill and welding ability (or knows someone who has) can fabricate a half decent stand provided that the pre-requisites at the beginning of the Chapter are followed. Additionally, a small pinch of improvisation and ingenuity could find you press ganging other items into use as gong stands – clothing racks from department stores or the smaller versions sold for home use have regularly been used as gong stands!

6.2   MALLETS, BEATERS, FLUMI AND STICKS

Unless you just want a gong as an *object d'art* you will need some form of beater or mallet (and probably a selection thereof) to play the gong. There is a wealth of different mallets from various manufacturers specifically for gongs but there are also beaters and sticks for other percussion instruments that could be used for playing the gong, all bringing out different sounds and timbres beyond the basic fundamental tone of your gong. These include bass drum mallets, vibraphone and marimba beaters and, although it causes me great pain to say this, metal triangle beaters...

The terms 'mallet', 'beater' and 'stick' are interchangeable and are used indiscriminately by players and manufacturers alike. As a *general* rule, a mallet is large, heavy and padded, a beater is medium size, medium weight and may or may not be padded, and a stick is long, thin, lightweight with no padding. But just to confuse, triangle beaters are actually metal sticks and tubular bell mallets are hard wood or plastic with no padding!

One mallet or beater that you should have above all others is a heavy, fleece covered mallet to bring out the warm fundamental note of your gong. This mallet should, where possible, be matched to the size of your gong. Too small and you only get the higher overtones and little 'weight' to the sound. Too large and the sound literally becomes smothered as too much of the surface area comes into contact with the gong thereby deadening it. Both Paiste and Chalklin grade their gong mallets to particular gong diameters, whereas other manufacturers tend to generalise with descriptions of 'suitable for 'small', 'medium' or 'large' gongs'.

Once you have this main mallet, you can add others to your collection. Smaller mallets can bring out the higher overtones and wool-wound mallets can make a gong 'speak' more quickly. As an orchestral percussionist, you will need a range of mallets to suit the requirements of the music – from a full bodied crash at the end of a Mahler symphony or the 'roar' effect found in Stravinsky's *The Rite of Spring*.

This Section looks at the mallets and beaters commonly available from a range of manufacturers. There are many others not covered, and you could make your own if so inclined. One final point – the term 'mallet' is used in its percussion form, a large beater with fleece-covered or wool-wound head. It does not refer to a wooden hammer used to knock tent pegs into the ground!

6.2.1 Paiste Mallets

As the world's largest producer of high quality gongs, one would expect Paiste to offer a complimentary range of high quality mallets and this is indeed the case. My earliest recollections (late 1970s) of Paiste mallets were a range of wooden-handled, hard compacted grey felt headed devices that didn't quite bring out the full sound of the gong and had an accompanying 'stick' noise, a term I use to describe the sound made when a stick or beater actually strikes the instrument.

By the mid 1980s Paiste had contracted the British firm of Chalklin to make a range of mallets and beaters specially designed and weighted to bring out the best sounds and timbres of their gongs. The original

Chalklin mallets had a 'square' head (i.e. diameter similar to depth) which had a hard compacted felt and plastic core. This was then fixed to an aluminium shaft and a thin leather thong was added at the end for hanging on a stand. The design was refined in the mid 1990s with a more spherical head, the fleece being attached by a screw at the top of the head and a plastic collar where it met the shaft. The shaft was slightly longer and powder-coated with a dark brown paint.

In more recent years, Paiste have switched to the German manufacturer SONA who use a very similar design to the later Chalklin design. The heads of the SONA mallets are slightly smaller but slightly heavier. For instance a 1980s M6 mallet by Chalklin has a head that measures 12cm wide by 11cm deep and weighs 500g whereas the SONA equivalent has a head 10cm by 10cm and weighs 550g. The brown powder-coated aluminium shaft still exists, but the hanging loop is now cord.

The SONA mallet is constructed using a hard, dense plastic core similar in shape to a beer barrel. Around this is wrapped several layers of cotton waste felt. The aluminium handle is fixed into a hole drilled into the plastic with a felt wedge and glue. The head is then encased in a white fleece 'sock' which is secured in place with a plastic collar where it meets the shaft and a plate and screw cap on top of the head. The handle is finished with a small PVC end cap and hanging cord.

The 'MX' coding developed by Paiste and Chalklin remains with the SONA mallets. This enables Paiste to suggest the best mallet for each of their gongs to bring out the best (fundamental) note and sound. The current list (2011) is as follows:-

Mallet M1	16"/41cm Symphonic Gong
	15"/38cm – 22"/56cm Tuned Gong
	No. 8, 9, 10 Sound Creation Gong
Mallet M2	20"/51cm Symphonic Gong
	18"/45cm – 24"/61cm Tuned Gong
	No. 2, 8 Sound Creation Gong

Mallet M3	22"/56cm – 24"/61cm Symphonic Gong
	24"/61cm Planet Gong
	No. 4, 5, 7, 9 Sound Creation Gong
Mallet M4	No. 1, 3, 6, 10 Sound Creation Gong
Mallet M5	26"/66cm – 30"/91cm Symphonic Gong
	26"/66cm – 30"/91cm Planet Gong
	26"/66cm – 30"/91cm Tuned Gong
Mallet M6	32"/81cm – 36"/91cm Symphonic Gong
	32"/81cm – 36"/91cm Planet Gong
	32"/81cm – 36"/91cm Tuned Gong
	No. 3a Sound Creation Gong
Mallet M7	38"/96cm – 50"/125cm Symphonic Gong
	38"/96cm Planet Gong
	No. 3b Sound Creation Gong
Mallet M8	60"/150cm Symphonic Gong
	No. 3c Sound Creation Gong
Mallet M8a	80"/205cm Symphonic Gong
Mallet M9	13"/33cm – 16"/40cm Tuned Gong
Mallet M10	9"/24cm – 12"/30cm Tuned Gong
Mallet M11	6"/15cm – 8.5"/22cm Tuned Gong
Mallet M12	For 'Bell Plates'

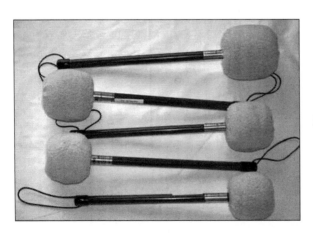

Paiste gong mallets made by SONA (M1, M2, M3, M5, M6)

Some of the MX range is not detailed here as they are designed for other instruments in the Paiste range such as crotales, bell plates and cymbals. Although each gong has a specified beater, there is absolutely no need to rigidly adhere to the suggested table. Smaller mallets can bring out other tones and higher fundamentals. Personally, I like to use the size below the recommended size e.g. a M5 mallet in place of a M6 mallet just to give a slightly less muffled sound. Some of the smaller beaters in the MX range can be used for tuned gongs or Himalayan Singing Bowls, and the M9 and M12 beaters are particularly useful ones to have in your collection. These beaters have a rubber core and are wrapped with a nylon/acrylic yarn. They make the gong 'splash' or 'speak' much quicker than fleece mallets and bring out higher overtones rather than the low fundamental. They are very useful for 'accenting' strokes.

6.2.2 SONA Mallets

In addition to making gong mallets for Paiste, SONA produce their own versions. The main difference is that SONA mallets have wooden handles (which are longer than the aluminium equivalent found on the version made for Paiste), with colour-coded end caps but no hanging cord. The handles are straight and there are ten fleece covered heads and one wool-wound head. The design of the head is very similar to the Paiste mallet, unsurprisingly.

The mallets are categorised by weight with a GM–XX coding:-

Mallet Number	Wool/Fleece	Weight
GM01	wool wound	135g
GM02	fleece	240g
GM03	fleece	320g
GM04	fleece	370g
GM05	fleece	460g
GM06	fleece	500g
GM07	fleece	590g
GM08	fleece	850g
GM09	fleece	900g
GM10	fleece	1050g
GM11	fleece	1300g

6.2.3 Chalklin Mallets

This British firm, founded in the 1970s by Richard Chalklin, is one of the largest manufacturers of percussion sticks and mallets in the world. They make a huge range of mallets and sticks for many percussion instruments such as keyboard (xylophone, marimba, glockenspiel, vibraphone), timpani, bass drum, cymbals, triangles, bells and gongs/tam-tams. Within individual percussion types, there are several different sets of beaters to choose from. For instance, in the timpani range, there are seven different sets with at least four pairs of sticks per set.

The gong and tam-tam mallets come in two ranges plus an additional two beaters to supplement the collection. The ranges are the 'TT' range (standing for Tam-Tam) and the 'GM' range (standing for Gong Mallet) though both ranges can be used for either type of instrument.

The TT range consists of five mallets numbered TT0 to TT4 covering very small (20"/50cm), small, medium, large and extra large (38"/95cm) gongs and roughly equate to the M3 to M6 Paiste mallets. They are of a similar construction, unsurprisingly, as Chalklin used to make gong mallets for Paiste. The handles are brown powder-coated aluminium with a hard foam grip end cap and a cord hanging loop. The head is 'over square' meaning that the depth is greater than the diameter, and is fleece-covered, though the fleece is a slightly thinner fabric than the Paiste variety meaning the head is slightly harder. This is good for making the gong 'speak' slightly quicker but is not as harsh as a wool wound mallet from other manufacturers. The fabric is normally a cream/beige colour but Chalklin has made the odd 'special' colour for people such as red or black. Price wise, they are significantly cheaper than a Paiste equivalent, at one point being nearly half price.

TT0 – suitable for gong diameter 20"/51cm – 22"/56cm

TT1 – suitable for gong diameter 24"/61cm – 26"/66cm

TT2 – suitable for gong diameter 28"/71cm – 32"/81cm

TT3 – suitable for gong diameter 34"/86cm – 36"/91cm

TT4 – suitable for gong diameter 38"/96cm – 40"/102cm

An additional beater in this range is the TT00. This mallet has a very small cream fleece head and thin aluminium shaft. It is ideal for bringing out high harmonics on a larger gong, and a pair of them are useful for doing rolls on the gong.

The GM range differs from the TT range in that the mallets have wooden handles and a head that is 'under square', i.e. the diameter is greater than the depth of the head. The heads are of similar construction to the TT range, fleece-covered and, to me at least, more carefully balanced. In many ways, I prefer using a GM mallet for orchestral works needing a Paiste Symphonic Gong.

The range consists of six mallets coded GM1 to GM6, essentially covering the Paiste M1 – M6 range in their suitability for a particular gong diameter.

GM1 – suitable for gong diameter   20"/51cm – 22"/56cm
GM2 – suitable for gong diameter   24"/61cm – 30"/76cm
GM3 – suitable for gong diameter   28"/71cm – 32"/81cm
GM4 – suitable for gong diameter   32"/81cm – 34"/86cm
GM5 – suitable for gong diameter   36"/91cm – 38"/96cm
GM6 – suitable for gong diameter   40"/102cm

Chalklin Gong Mallets (l-r TT3, TT2, TT00, WG2, GM2, GM3, GM5)

The TG1 and WG2 mallets are special additions to the range. They consist of a rubber core, wool-wound head on an aluminium handle, and are analogous to the Paiste M9 and M12 mallets. The TG1 is intended for tuned gongs, especially Thai/Burmese gongs whereas the WG2 is intended to bring out the best in Wind gongs. They can also be used for accenting strokes on any gong.

6.2.4 Vic Firth Mallets

The American Vic Firth is a percussionist of international acclaim and is mostly recognised for his wide range of percussion sticks, beaters and mallets. To me, he is the American 'Chalklin'. Within the

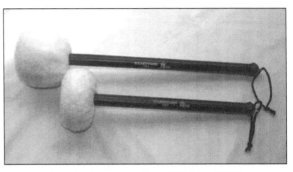

Vic Firth gong mallets (GM1, GM2)

range there are four types of gong mallet and these have been developed more with the Chao gong in mind but are also suitable for other gong types.

The Soundpower™ Large Gong Beater (GM1) is a mallet made for large gongs from 30"/75cm to 50"/126cm diameters. It has a large diameter (4.5"/11cm) synthetic fleece-covered head and a hardwood handle approximately 21"/53cm long. It is very good for bringing out the low fundamental note and lower tones, though the head itself is not as heavy as a Paiste equivalent. This means that the player must use more strength and playing technique rather than the weight of the mallet to bring out the desired tone.

The Soundpower™ Small Gong Beater (GM2) is intended for smaller tam-tams, gamelan and tuned gongs. The head is a thin disc shape with a synthetic fleece cover and a 17"/43cm long hardwood handle. Disc-shaped gong mallets are rarely used in the UK but have found favour in the US and parts of Europe. I have seen both wood and metal disc heads with the edge surrounded by felt. They tend to make a tam-tam 'speak' quicker with a more pronounced hard fundamental note and a more instantaneous 'crash'. The Vic Firth model is the first I have seen where the head is entirely covered in fur or felt. Most disc type beaters just have the striking surface covered.

The Soundpower™ Heavy Gong Beater (GB3) is similar in style to the Paiste M12 and Chalklin WG2 mallets, except the head is bigger. The head (3.5"/9cm diameter) has a large rubber core which is tightly wound with wool/yarn. Intended for a full sound at all dynamics, it can make a gong speak more quickly than a fleece-covered mallet, though the yarn on this mallet gives a little so it appears less strident than similar mallets.

The GB3's smaller brother is the GB4 Soundpower™ Medium Gong Beater which still has a rubber core, yarn-wound head, though somewhat smaller and with a diamond shaped cross section.

GB1 – suitable for gong diameter   30"/76cm – 50"/127cm

GB2 - suitable for gong diameter   22"/56cm – 28"/71cm

GB3 – suitable for gong diameter   34"/86cm – 50"/127cm

GB4 – suitable for gong diameter   28"/71cm – 40"/102cm

6.2.5 Sabian

Sabian have two gong mallets in their catalogue. These are of the fleece-covered variety rather than yarn wound as preferred by other manufacturers on the North American continent. In previous catalogues Sabian offered several size of gong mallet based on the disc shaped head. These were a metal (possibly aluminium) core with the edge covered in a black felt.

The current Sabian Small Pro Gong Mallet has a 3 ¾"/9.5cm diameter head and a 19"/48cm long hardwood handle. The fleece is black and the mallet is intended for 24"/61cm to 30"/76cm gongs.

The Sabian Large Pro Gong Mallet has a larger head of 4 ¼"/11cm diameter with a similar length hardwood handle and black fleece covering. This mallet is intended for gongs ranging from 36"/91cm to 52"/132cm diameter.

6.2.6 Mike Balter

Mike Balter, a well known American percussionist from Chicago, has also developed a wide range of beaters, sticks and mallets for all sorts of instruments. His gong mallet range comprises four models of the wool/yarn wound head type.

The GM1 mallet has a black yarn wound head which has a diamond shaped cross section, 3½"/9cm diameter with a 17"/43cm maple wood handle. The GM2 mallet is a heavier version with a brown yarn 3"/9.5cm diameter head and 17"/43cm long handle. No indication of their suitability to a particular gong size is given. The GM3 mallet has a small head, 3"/7.5cm diameter wound in a light grey yarn and shorter handle. This is meant for smaller gongs or accenting strokes. The WG1 mallet is intended for Wind gongs with a 2"/5cm head wound in blue yarn. All handles are made from maple and are covered at one end with a vinyl plastic grip.

Mike Balter mallet (top), Yamaha mallet (bottom)

6.2.7 Yamaha

Yamaha are a large manufacturer of musical instruments and percussion instruments. They don't make gongs or cymbals, nor do they 'brand' other manufacturers' instruments. They do make a wide range of beaters which include gong mallets of the yarn-wound head variety.

The Artist Master™ gong mallet range consists of three models. They all have 1"/2.5cm thick maple shafts around 17"/43cm long with a yarn wound solid (rubber) core heads. The 'YGM-1' is for light use, the 'YGM-2' is a general purpose gong mallet, and the 'YGM-3' is a heavier mallet meant for bringing out the fuller sound of a gong or for use on larger diameter gongs.

6.2.8 Chinese Mallets

Most gongs bought from China, or via a dealer importing from China, come with a mallet or beater. Unfortunately, these tend not to be that high quality. They are usually made from wood, with the head being wound in cotton tape – the thicker the tape, the more cushioned the beater head. The tape is usually secured in place under a metal or plastic cap. They are either 'hard' or 'very hard' and do not bring out the full depth and warmth of the gong, though they reflect the more rhythmic playing style used with Chinese gongs. They are useful for effects such as accenting

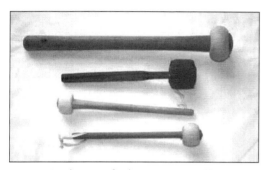

A selection of Chinese gong mallets

and are very good for striking Himalayan Singing Bowls and small tuned gongs. Many importers indicate five different sizes of beaters being available, though I and others have collected many different types, including some with soft felt heads.

6.2.9 Flumi

The flumi is said to be a German invention and is a rubber or vulcanised plastic ball (sometimes referred to as a 'Superball') mounted onto a stick. When dragged across the face of a gong, it produces all sorts of weird and wonderful squeaks, groans and sonic sounds that people have variously described as Gregorian chanting, Buddhist monk intoning, whale and dolphin song, and choirs of angels. This spacey and ethereal sound is used to great effect in sound healing, though the effect is occasionally used in *avant-garde* music (e.g. Stockhausen) and the odd film score.

Many sound healing shops and websites sell them but it is very easy to make your own. Simply drill a small hole of the diameter of your stick half way into the ball and then glue in your stick. The surface of the ball should be roughened slightly with emery paper to allow the ball to grip the surface of the gong. Once dry, try out the flumi on your gong (grip the stick near the ball) by dragging it across various

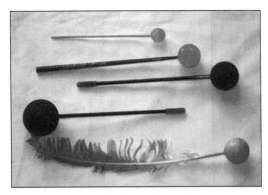

a selection of Flumi

surfaces in different directions. Try different sizes of ball as well. One of the best sounds I ever made with a flumi was by using one with a well worn head the size of a thumb nail on a Paiste 60" Symphonic Gong. The quiet, spacey whistle drifted off into an infinite space that seemed to exist at the back of the gong. Very moving!

When you have finished using a flumi on a gong, wipe the gong face with a soft brush or cloth as the ball leaves rubber streaks on the face which become harder to clean off the longer you leave them.

6.2.10 Metal beaters

I suppose, for completeness, I ought to discuss the use of metal beaters on gongs. I will state right now that I am completely against the use of metal beaters on gongs. Personally it is a sound completely out of character for the instrument and probably the best way of damaging it. Remember, metal hammers were used to make the instruments and they left their mark!

The use of metal beaters has its origin in Stravinsky's most famous work – *The Rite of Spring*. An excellent piece of music for the tam-tam and its player, at several points in the music it involves the use of a metal beater being drawn around the rim or across the face of the tam-tam producing a 'zinging' sound which is quite primeval and is probably why it is used in this way. The Paiste Symphonic Gong gives the best results due to its bumpy hammered surface. This sound, however, is not that loud, hence the humble triangle beater (which is often used) tends to get morphed into a larger metal stick to give the necessary volume to cut through the loud music in this section. Unfortunately I have seen some quite horrific ways of producing the necessary sound. I saw a member of the New York Philharmonic dragging a steel beater across the face of their tam-tam at a concert in London and I saw a performance by the Concertgebouw Orchestra of Amsterdam where the percussionist drags *two* triangles across the face of their Chao tam-tam! The score calls for the use of a metal beater so all I can suggest is take care! Try running the beater on the inner rim of the tam-tam and try using a Chalklin brass-tipped triangle beater then you are at least scraping together similar metals.

The other use of metal beaters on gongs is to produce a rhythmic pattern such as that found in the first dance of Shchedrin's 'Carmen Suite'. This appears, to me, a pointless exercise which can easily be mimicked by the use of a wooden drum stick or nylon-tipped wooden drum stick for tapping out the rhythm on the gong. Most of the rest of the orchestra are playing the same rhythm, so it begs the question – what is the point of damaging your gong for an effect that cannot really be heard, except by you?

6.3   CASES AND BAGS

If you intend to carry or move your gong around, you need to invest in a decent quality case or bag for it. When I bought my first gong 25 years ago, the only things that were available in the UK were cymbal bags or the Le Blond range of cases. One player I knew kept his gong in a case made from plywood and wooden battens!

In more recent times there has been a big increase in the number of bags and cases available. Many of these have been born out of requirements from percussionists and drummers so it is to these manufacturers and stockists that one must go to source suitable cases and bags. Whether you choose a bag or a case is up to you. Bags have the advantage of being lightweight, padded, and easily folded for storage. Cases have a certain stiffness that allows for shock loading and things being stacked on top of them, but conversely, cases can be bulky and take up more room than a bag.

6.3.1 Mushroom Covers

First and foremost for gong bags are those made by Tony Lucas and Mushroom Covers. Since 1988 Tony has developed a range of covers for large percussion instruments, such as timpani and bass drums, that afford a large degree of protection to these instruments than was hitherto available. The covers were made from vinyl-covered foam that snugly fits the instrument and can also be easily cleaned.

The gong bags are made from a nylon fabric outer and inner layer with a foam layer sandwiched in between. Two robust handles allow the gong to be carried vertically, and two heavy duty zips going round almost the entire circumference of the bag, allow the bag to be completely zipped open and the gong laid carefully inside rather than it being slid in, though this is still an option by just unzipping to half the circumference. The bags are made to order for most sizes of gong but cymbal bags of 22" and 24" diameter are frequently available. Delivery time is about 4 to 6 weeks. The bags may seem expensive compared to Chinese versions, but the quality is very good and so they are my bag of choice. They are available from JAM Percussion in the UK.

6.3.2 Protection Racket

This UK firm based in Cornwall has for the past 20 years made bags and cases for the drummer. Their gong bags are made in a similar way to their cymbal bags. They have a nylon fabric outer with a fleece-lined inner and a tough nylon zip. The deluxe cymbal bag has straps and webbing so that it can be carried on your back. The 24" cymbal bag can fit 24" diameter gongs. Larger gong bags can be made to order.

6.3.3 Chinese Gong Bags

Available from a variety of sound healing gong suppliers, these budget bags are made in China and are good value for money. They are a nylon fabric with a foam sandwich and have a zip, carrying handles and shoulder straps. They are deep and can carry two or more gongs providing you use suitable inserts between the gongs to stop them scratching each other. They are available in a number of sizes.

6.3.4 Cymbal Manufacturers/Suppliers

For gongs up to 24" in diameter, it is worth looking at bags produced by the major cymbal manufacturers or suppliers. Paiste, Zildjian, Sabian, Meinl, UFIP and Stagg all have their own branded cymbal bags, normally for cymbals up to 22" diameter, but occasionally up to 24" diameter. Most drum/percussion shops have these in stock at very reasonable prices.

6.3.5 Le Blond

One of the best known percussion case makers, this UK based firm has been making cases for drums, cymbals, gongs and 'hardware' for many years. They are the only major source of hard cases for gongs larger than 24" in the UK, unless you have another maker custom build one for you.

The cases are made from a lightweight polypropylene material, though earlier cases may have been made from a vulcanised rubber/plastic. They consist of an almost circular base with a flat edge to allow them to stand on this edge when vertical. The side is riveted to the base. The lid is thinner than the base and its edge is also riveted to the lid top. There is a carrying handle in solid plastic at the top edge of the case and webbing straps with spring clips hold the lid to the base. There is no padding inside the case so I recommend that the gong is wrapped in a cotton sheet before placing it in the case. When the lid and base are separate, the case becomes quite flexible which means that it has to be placed flat on the ground to load up the gong. In the confines of a concert hall, especially when packing away, people often inadvertently stand in the case of a large gong, leaving dusty footprints, which scratches the gong. My 38" Paiste Symphonic tam-tam suffered from 15 years of such treatment so that the raised hammer marks on its face bear numerous small scratches. I now wrap the gong in Egyptian cotton sheets to prevent further deterioration.

The cases are rigid once the top is strapped on and this allows other instruments to be stacked on top without damage to the gong. My case is often the first to be loaded into my car with a bass drum or cymbal cases loaded on top. It has lasted 15 years which is testament to the quality of the cases.

Le Blond also make a range of 'hardware' cases, designed for stands for drums and cymbals, but they also make excellent cases to carry round your mallets, beaters and singing bowls. They have also introduced liners for some of their smaller cases so it will be interesting to see if ones can be made for gong cases in future.

6.3.6 Hardcase

You could say that this UK firm based in Derbyshire does exactly what it says on their tin! Another firm established about 20 years ago, they produce cases for drummers and their paraphernalia, plus cases for equipment for the wider music industry. They make gong cases from a high impact resistant polyethylene and in sizes from 20" to 30" with other sizes to special order.

6.3.7 Humes and Berg

Humes and Berg is an American firm which was established in Chicago, Indiana in 1935. They began by making mutes for brass instruments but expanded to make cases for practically all musical instruments. They use

A selection of cases and bags – Le Blond case (rear), Mushroom Covers (front l), Chinese bag (front r).

a variety of materials from vulcanised fibre to leather. The gong cases are made from vulcanised fibre and can be ordered with liners (Enduro range) or without liners (Fiber range). They also produce a gong bag from vinyl and foam called the Tuxedo range. Bags and cases are available for 20" to 40" diameter gongs.

7 CARE AND MAINTENANCE OF GONGS

A gong is both a musical instrument and a healing instrument. As we have seen, some cultures believe them to be possessed by spirits, a way of communicating with the spirit world, or even with God! You will most certainly have invested a substantial sum of money in your gong, hence you owe it to yourself to look after it. This Chapter covers some of the damage that can occur to a gong and ways of avoiding it, plus a look at ways of cleaning the gong.

7.1 DAMAGE

Essentially a gong can be damaged in a number of ways: −

Scratches

Dents

Cracks

Corrosion

'Metal fatigue'

7.1.1 Scratches

It is a fact of life that at some point your gong will get scratched no matter how hard you try to avoid it. A scratch in itself will not affect the tone or sound of the gong, only its looks, but repairing the scratch could do more harm than good. Small light surface scratches can be polished out to a certain extent but scratches that you can feel when you rub your thumb or finger nail over them cannot be removed without seriously affecting the sound of the gong. You can at least minimise the chances of scratching gongs by adopting some or all of the following good practices:-

Consider removing rings, watches and other jewellery. Before you pick up your gong and use it, consider removing jewellery that can impact the gong during handling. Wedding and engagement rings are a great source of scratches especially if that hand is used for damping the gong.

Dust and grit on mallets. How many of you put your mallets and beaters on the floor of a concert hall, church hall or therapy room without any form of protection between the floor and the mallet? It is so easy to pick up dust and grit from these floors, not just due to the direct contact with the material, but also due to the electrostatic nature of manmade fibres. You then pick up the mallet and play the gong, grinding the dust and grit into the surface as you play, or swirl it around the gong face as you use the mallet to dampen the gong. To avoid this, try using a sheepskin or alpaca skin fleece on the floor and lay your mallets and beaters on this. The fleeces can be shaken or washed after each session and their natural fibres do not become electrostatically charged. It is also a good idea to physically check your mallets for any dust or grit by slapping the mallet against the open palm of your hand and running your hand quite firmly over the head of the mallet to tease out any grit.

Buckles, buttons and necklaces. These items can come into contact with the gong when hanging it, lifting it out of a case, or any manoeuvre where the gong could touch your body. The tip here is that for those of you who keep your gongs in a bag, just unzip the bag enough to expose the gong cord/gut then lift the gong and bag and hang it on the stand. Once in place, unzip the bag fully and peel away the bag. When taking the gong down from the stand, just reverse the above.

Long finger nails. Cut them!

7.1.2 Corrosion

Once a gong has left the factory it will be subject to corrosive forces regardless of wax or lacquer protective coatings. These coatings will stem the rate of corrosion, but wax coatings in particular are relatively easy to remove. Corrosion of gongs takes place in two ways – from liquids in contact with the gong (water, sweat, drinks etc) and the atmosphere (humidity, smoke, aerosols etc.) Water attacks copper, tin and nickel in the metal to form hydrated oxides of these metals. These manifest themselves as black or green markings in the metal and pitting in the metal surface. Sweat is particularly nasty as it contains salts as well as water thereby increasing the corrosiveness. Water vapour in the air has the same effect and oxygen causes the metal to oxidise and tarnish, dulling the metal. There isn't a great deal to be done about water vapour and oxygen as this is present in the atmosphere but we can dry our hands before touching a gong and keep away colleagues who smoke, who are drinking bottled water, or worse, cola drinks! I have also heard a story about one gong healing practitioner who, at the end of a session, kissed her gong! This eventually led to some corrosion and pitting on the face of the gong. Fortunately most of the discolouration was reversed by cleaning and polishing but the pitting remained. In my collection, I have two of the five Symphonic Gongs given to the Ludwig Drum Company by Paiste when they became the distributer for Paiste products in the USA during the 1960s. There was quite a lot of water damage to these gongs and both needed a weekend's worth of cleaning and polishing to restore some sort of cleanliness to them.

Cleaning of gongs is covered later in this chapter but if a gong gets wet, dry it thoroughly. If the wetness is due to anything else but pure water, wash the gong with mild soap and water and then dry thoroughly.

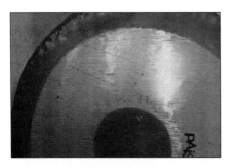

corrosion marks on
Paiste Symphonic Gong

corrosion marks on rear face of
Paiste Symphonic Gong

7.1.3 Dents

Dents are caused in two ways – by the gong swinging into or being dropped onto a hard object, or by something heavy and hard being dropped onto, or knocking into, the gong. Gongs made from sheet bronze and nickel silver (e.g Paiste, Meinl, UFIP) and thin cast gongs (Wind Gongs, UFIP Targo tam-tam, Chinese opera gongs) are at a higher risk from dents than a Chao gong. A Chao gong is made from thicker metal so it doesn't dent as easily, but it can get gouged, cracked, or even shatter if it is dropped, or something bangs into it.

Once a gong has received a dent, it is very hard to remove. The metal has become compressed at the point of impact and stretched around the impact point. To repair it, the affected area needs to be re-heated and re-hammered which will invariably alter the tuning of the gong. Any such repair can only be done by a skilled gong smith, but I am not aware of any of the major manufacturers offering such a service. Essentially, once the gong is dented, it's there for life. Prevention is definitely better than cure. The worst example I have seen of a dent in a gong was on the Paiste tam-tam used by the Royal Liverpool Philharmonic Orchestra in the 1980s where someone had struck the gong (with a large mallet) full force with a straight on blow rather than a glancing blow (see playing techniques). This large dent was quite easily seen from the auditorium and the gong spent the following season being played from the rear during concerts in a vain attempt to try and reverse the damage. It was ultimately replaced by a 38" Paiste Symphonic Gong but the fundamental of this new gong was higher in pitch than the old gong, so this new gong passed to me and is now my main orchestral tam-tam.

7.1.4 Cracks

Cracks occur as a result of impact damage from dropping metal or sharp objects onto the gong, by playing the gong too vigorously with hard sticks, or by the gong impacting an unyielding surface. They tend to occur on the rim but can occur on the face. I have a Burmese gong with a V-shaped crack on the face, roughly halfway between the boss and the rim. Cracks can be seen by carefully inspecting the gong but hairline cracks are more difficult to detect. A crack can often announce itself audibly by a sort of 'zinging' sound whilst it is being played. This should not be confused by the metallic buzz that comes from a Paiste gong when the ends of the gut cord rub against the underside of the rim or rear face.

A crack cannot be repaired. You can only try and prevent it from spreading. This process involves drilling a small hole at either end of the crack with a very sharp high speed steel drill bit, proceeding carefully to avoid heat built up. It should only be attempted by people with good engineering skills and the right tools, and there is no guarantee of success. There is also a chance that the drilling process can cause new hairline cracks. If the crack is in the face of the gong, both ends of the crack will need to be drilled. Some people have even resorted to removing a whole piece of the gong. I played in a concert in 1986 where a gong from the Royal Northern College of Music (in the UK) was being used. It had a circular hole several centimetres in diameter which had been cut just off centre in the face of the gong, which had been done for this reason.

Again, none of the major manufacturers offer a repair service, and if the crack cannot be repaired, then the gong really needs pensioning off to a much more gentle life of *piano* and *mezzo piano* sounds. Welding cannot be used as it is very difficult to weld nickel silver or bronze, and the intense heat will change the tuning and stress the metal. Some South-East Asian gong makers have developed the use of resinous pastes to repair cracks and holes but this is a closely guarded secret and does not seem to have been successfully used in the West. Brazing techniques have also been used to limited effect.

7.1.5 Metal Fatigue

Although 'metal fatigue' covers a whole range of problems with a metals' strength, malleability and ductility, I am using it here to describe a particular problem that affects sheet metal gongs. It can be quite hard to detect, especially when one is familiar with the 'crashy' overtones of a Paiste or UFIP tam-tam, but it is this splashy overtone that can indicate the onset of metal fatigue. Essentially the fundamental note of the gong becomes less pronounced and the higher partials and overtones 'speak' far quicker than normal.

It is caused by playing the gong too hard – *fortissimo* strokes all the time, loud rolls, or trying to make a small gong sound like something much bigger. Audible examples include recordings of classical music by the City of Birmingham Symphony Orchestra (CBSO) in the late 1960s and 70s. Try some of the recordings of Malcolm Arnold's symphonies and notice how 'tinny' the tam-tam sounds. The CBSO ultimately replaced this tam-tam with a Wuhan tam-tam for a decade or so. Another classic example is the loud tam-tam stroke at the end of the video for Queen's Bohemian Rhapsody. This is quite a tinny sounding crash, especially when one sees the size of the instrument that Roger Taylor strikes – in the same manner as the man on the Rank Organisation gong.

Gongs played by rock bands and brass bands are quite prone to metal fatigue as they are often overplayed. This can be prevented by miking up the gong for a rock gig so it doesn't have to be overplayed, or by firmly refusing a conductor's request to 'play up' when your 28" tam-tam cannot possibly emulate the larger 38" tam-tam of the professional symphony orchestra.

What is actually happening in 'metal fatigue' is that the metal crystals that have been tightly compacted and aligned in the crystal lattice during the rolling process are beginning to pull apart, allowing the molecules to vibrate more freely and lose cohesion. It cannot be cured short of melting and re-rolling the metal.

7.2   CLEANING GONGS

If we were discussing the cleaning of cymbals we would find a wealth of information, suggestions and tips. We would also find a wealth of conflicting advice – for every suggestion there is usually contradicting advice. We would also find a range of cleaning solutions and pastes made by the manufacturers themselves – Zildjian, Sabian and Paiste all produce cymbal cleaners, and whilst a manufacturer would not sell you a product that would damage their cymbals, they should only be used on their cymbals. It's worth remembering that these cleaners have been produced for bronze cymbals, so whilst they may be fine for Chinese bronze Chao and Wind gongs, they may not be suitable for the nickel silver gongs of Paiste, SONA, Meinl etc.

Information on cleaning gongs is, at the time of writing, fairly limited. Hopefully this will increase in future as various gong forums become more popular. There is some good advice on Michael Bettine's website in the US (www.gongtopia.com/lessons) and the US gong retailer Gongs Unlimited have written an article about gong cleaning in their newsletter (www.gongs-unlimited.com). Later in this Section I have detailed my own preferred method for cleaning gongs which is based on a method used by gong master Sheila Whittaker here in the UK, with an additional step for cleaning engrained dirt that I have devised.

When cleaning a gong, one needs to decide on the depth of the cleaning. If it is just to remove dust, fingerprints, flumi marks or spilt liquids then the best way is to clean it with warm water and soap. Some people put a splash of lemon juice in the water to help it 'cut' through some of the dirt. Either way, the gong must be dried thoroughly to avoid corrosion from residual water. Also take care with the temperature of the water. Hot or boiling water will alter the temper of the metal and could risk cracking the gong. If you are looking to remove engrained dirt or restore a shine then another cleaning technique needs to be used. Again, ask the question 'what level of cleaning?' Some gong enthusiasts think that the ageing patina on the gong adds to its character. If you agree with this, then just clean occasionally with soap and water plus the odd dusting.

Before considering other cleaning techniques, you need to be aware of the gongs factory finish. Paiste, Meinl and SONA gongs have a wax polish put on which will eventually be removed by various cleaning techniques. UFIP gongs have a lacquer coating which means they only really need dusting or washing with soap and water. Any mechanical or chemical cleaning product will remove this lacquer allowing the gong surface to oxidise. South-East Asian and Chao gongs have an oxidised surface, which is part of the decoration, so unless you want to permanently remove this, it is best left alone.

Products for cleaning and polishing metals tend to work in one of two ways. Firstly there is the mechanical abrading technique where tiny particles of abrading material (often chalk) grind out the dirt from the micropores of the metal surface. They also grind away the metal itself and the larger the particle size, the more aggressive the metal removal. The second method involves a chemical reaction to unstick the dirt and grime from the metal surface and thereby de-oxidise the elemental metal back to a purer form. The main chemicals tend to be Ammonia (used for centuries as a cleaning agent) and sodium hydroxide (caustic soda). These are aggressive chemicals even in dilute form, and will react quite happily with copper, tin and nickel to potentially damage your gong rather than clean it. To this end, all household cleaners should be avoided, including bleach, toilet cleaner, bathroom/sink cleaners, scouring powder etc. Also that household favourite Brasso™ should not be used as it contains ammonia. Solvents can also be found in cleaning products used to dissolve grease etc. but they can also react with wax coatings or lacquers so should be used with care.

Some success has been reported with silver polishes such as Silvo™ and Goddards Silver Polish™ (my favourite) which are both good for bringing out the shine on any gong. Don't use the dipping solution versions of these products as too much chemical reaction takes place which will discolour or damage the gong. Other sources report some success with automotive cleaning products such as paint restorer and wax polishes. The paint restorers can remove faint scratches and marks. This is essentially what they do to dull car body paintwork – cutting back the dull oxidised paint to its original colour and then using a good quality polish/wax to protect the paint and enhance its shine. Again, use the best you can afford such as the Autoglym™ range of products. If it's good enough for an Aston Martin, it's good enough for your gong! The use of a sealing automotive wax or high quality furniture wax polish is recommended to prolong the new shine on that clean surface that you have spent so much effort in achieving. Paiste use a product called 'Bohrer Wax' to seal their gongs.

Whatever cleaning method you use, start by cleaning a small area on the rear of the gong just in case something goes wrong. Work in small areas at a time and don't leave any cleaning product on the gong for more than a few minutes before cleaning it off. Always hand polish, never use powered buffing or polishing tools as the heat generated from this process will affect the temper and tuning of the gong. Finally, take extra care when cleaning Paiste and Meinl gongs. That brown colour on the rim and in the centre which readily identifies these gongs can be removed by some cleaners and vigorous rubbing! I have seen one very anaemic-looking tuned gong that had been over cleaned!

7.3 MY METHOD FOR CLEANING GONGS

Disclaimer: Before starting I just want to say that the method described here works for me, but I take no responsibility whatsoever for any damage to anyone's gong so caused by using this method.

Start by using a Cape Cod™ metal cleaning cloth – these cloths, available in the UK from Lakeland, have a cleaning solution impregnated into the cloth, which smells of vanilla pods. Rub the surface of the gong with both circular motions (around the face and back) and linear motions along any scraped patterns or decoration. The cloth will get very black in colour as it removes dirt and oxidised coatings. This is not a problem – you do not need to keep turning the cloth over to a clean bit or change it as long as the cloth remains moist. The surface of the gong will get very

black but don't worry at this stage -- just keep cleaning until the whole surface is complete. Now take a clean soft cloth (or terry towel) and clean off as much of the 'blackness' as possible. Don't worry if the gong now looks filthy. Just remove most of the excess polish off, frequently turning the cloth to a cleaner bit, then discard or wash the cloth.

Next step is to take some Goddards Silver Polish ™

Paiste Symphonic Gong following cleaning

(the one with a brick red polish and a sponge applicator), wet the sponge applicator, wring out, and apply some polish to the gong. Work in circles outwards from the centre and along any scraped features or tooling marks. Rinse the sponge frequently and apply polish sparingly. Once the polish has been applied all over the gong, rinse the sponge in clean water, wring out and then start to remove the polish with the sponge, rinsing it frequently. Do this for a second time with a change of water for your sponge. Wipe the gong dry with a clean terry towel and then buff the gong with a high quality microfibre polishing cloth of the type used to polish concours cars. If you wish, apply a little Autoglym™ resin polish to a cloth and quickly polish over the gong.

8. GONG PLAYING TECHNIQUES

In this Section we will look at some basic gong playing techniques. I've split it into two types – orchestral playing and sound healing. With orchestral players, the gong tends to be mounted on a stand that means it is at waist height and at the side of the player, who normally reaches down to the playing spot. For sound healers, the gong is usually mounted at chest level, regardless of whether the player is either standing or sitting, so the player faces the gong, either directly in front or off to one side. In either case both sections are relevant as the techniques can be used in either playing mode. For brass band players, drummers and the like, choose any technique that suits you, depending on whether your gong is 'high' mounted or 'low' mounted. As ever, what are described here are just some basic tips. As with playing any musical instrument, a good teacher is invaluable. Don't make the mistake that all you need to do is just hit the gong, there's more to it than that! Also, the tips described here are for 'tam-tams'. There is a separate short section on tuned gongs. For more tips on playing gongs, I can recommend the books by Mehab Benton[1] and Sheila Whittaker[2] and the short videos on the Vic Firth website[3].

Safety Note – gongs can be very noisy. When played really loudly they produce 'white noise' and can affect the hearing. If you suffer from tinnitus you may find even low volumes slightly painful. This is also important if you use gongs for Sound Healing and your client suffers from tinnitus, as you may have to moderate your style. Also, not everyone enjoys gongs being played loudly (though some do!) It is therefore worth considering some form of hearing protection such as ear plug(s) when you are playing. I often wear one in the left ear when playing in an orchestra or band as the tam-tam tends to be on my left side. This way

I can still hear the music but have a level of protection for my left ear during the loud moments.

8.1   ORCHESTRAL PLAYING TECHNIQUES

8.1.1   Positioning

The positioning of a tam-tam in orchestral playing is very much dependent upon how much space is available and who needs to play it – one person or several. Generally the percussion section tends to be placed at the back of the orchestra. With this assumption, the tam-tam is usually placed either parallel to the back of the stage (facing the conductor) or perpendicular (90°) to it (edge on to the conductor). Parallel to the back of the stage is visually pleasing to the audience and is a bit more out of the way, allowing other players to reach it easily, but from a playing point of view, it is not as easy, as you have to twist your upper body round to see the music and the conductor. This isn't a problem when the tam-tam is positioned perpendicular to the back of the stage. You are facing the music and conductor, but the placing of the instruments either side of the tam-tam needs thinking about due to the swing, accessibility, and the eardrums' of the woodwind or brass players in front of the tam-tam who are usually not very appreciative of a *fortissimo* stroke just behind their heads!

8.1.2 Basic Stroke

The basic stroke for *any* type of gong/tam-tam playing is a glancing or bounced blow from the mallet. It is not hit directly in a forward/back movement as this produces a poor quality sound, and there is a certain amount of deadening of the sound with this method, as the mallet remains in contact with the metal a little longer than a glanced blow. You are looking for that blossoming, warm sound *after* the mallet stroke has been struck. The striking point is roughly about half way between the centre of the tam-tam and its edge, usually in the 5, 6 or 7 o'clock position. On all tam-tams there is a so-called 'sweet spot' where the best quality sound will be produced from the instrument. It's in the area of the 5 to 7 o'clock segment of the face so have a play around to find the sweet spot on your gong. Also, you don't strike it in the centre as this does not give the blossoming sound you're after and in any case, the centre is considered the 'heart' of the tam-tam, so it's considered 'bad form' by many to strike the tam-tam here. Note, we always say 'strike', 'blow', 'tap' etc never 'hit'. 'Hitting' a gong is considered too violent, as it is not just an instrument to many but a spiritual artefact as well.

The basic stroke can be achieved either by bringing the mallet diagonally towards the front of the tam-tam and glancing off at an angle or by 'flicking' the wrist in an upward motion just as the mallet strikes. It is useful to also 'prime' the tam-tam by either softly tapping the instrument with the mallet or end of your finger. This has the effect of starting the metal molecules vibrating so that they are already energised before the main stroke arrives. If you don't prime the gong it means that it is struck 'cold' and the tone is less pleasing. Priming the gong is also a skill to master as you need to be able to do this without producing an audible note.

The weight needed to produce a definite level of sound is one of the hardest skills to master and this is where knowledge of the characteristics of the instrument, the mallets and the energy level of the tam-tam is invaluable. Far too many players underplay the tam-tam in an orchestra, something which annoys me intensely, especially when I've paid good money to hear a work that I am keen on! Part of this is due to the tam-tam being considered something you just hit, and not worthy of practice, and the other is a recognition that it can make a lot of noise and is sometimes difficult to control, hence a natural tendency to underplay. For amateur players, this is understandable. For the professionals, my expectations are somewhat higher. So get to know your instrument and its capabilities, nuances and shortcomings so you feel confident in placing the stroke correctly with the required weight.

For *piano* or quiet strokes, use your wrists and use small arm movements to produce the right volume. For louder notes, use more arm plus the weight of the mallet. For a *fortissimo* stroke (also called a thunderclap in the sound healing world) a strong glancing blow using the whole arm plus a flick of the wrist will produce a loud, clean crash, which is a joy to hear and produce. As you practice you will also note that different sounds can be obtained from the tam-tam depending where on the face you are playing, the angle of the mallet when it strikes the tam-tam, and the hardness or softness of the mallets you are using.

8.1.3   Repeated Notes

The score may call for a pulse on the tam-tam or a gradual build up of sound with a succession of single notes. The trick is to stop the subsequent strikes dampening the sound when this sort of playing is required. In addition, you need to control the volume without the sudden rush of sound that can occur with energy being fed into the tam-tam. In both cases this can usually be controlled by subtle damping of the instrument with either the mallet or the free hand. Damping will be discussed later.

8.1.4   Crescendo – Diminuendo Rolls

One of the best effects in orchestral tam-tam playing is the *crescendo* roll. Starting *pianissimo*, the instrument is repeatedly beaten and a swelling of sound emerges, culminating in an earth-shattering roar. This is a great effect and reasonably easy to achieve. There are two ways of obtaining a roll, one is to use a matched pair of beaters and rapidly alternate between the hands, the volume being produced by the rate of beating and how hard you are striking the tam-tam on each beat. A quick *crescendo* is usually produced by rapid beating and a greater arm movement. A slow *crescendo* can be the same but at a more relaxed pace. The advantage of using two beaters, in some people's view, is that there is less 'sticking note' (the sound of the beater or stick actually hitting the surface of an instrument, rather than the sound that the stick/beater produces from the instrument) and a smoother roll. The downside for orchestral playing is that you find yourself leaning over the instrument more if you are playing on one face, and it is then difficult to damp the noise in this position. It is also bad for your back due to the poor posture. The alternative is to alternately strike the front and rear faces though there is a small risk of the beaters cancelling themselves out if you are beating either side of the same spot.

For me and many others, using a single beater at the same point is far more preferable. It is easier to control and you have a free hand for damping purposes. As regards a more 'lumpy' roll, it doesn't matter. Only if the audience is sat immediately behind you will they notice the individual beats as you start. Once the drone is in motion, the higher partials will ring through and divert the ear to focus on this rush of the higher tones of the instrument. Whichever method you use, remember that you don't have to play the instrument for the entire length of the note(s) in the music. Stop before the written music notation does and let the inherent characteristic of the tam-tam, its ability to get louder *after* you stop playing, carry it through for the duration of the note in the part.

With a rolled *diminuendo*, this is often a misunderstanding on the part of the composer. The tam-tam naturally decays away as a *diminuendo* so let the instrument do this, again with careful use of damping as the score requires. Rolling a *diminuendo* note with a beater is a bit of a waste of effort.

A good piece to practice rolls and learning to control *crescendos* and *diminuendos* is 'Mars' from Holst's *The Planet Suite*. The gong part comprises several dozen bars of roll, gradually getting louder (with the odd *diminuendo*) until *fortississimo* is reached. Start by regular beating of the gong with one mallet. The beat should be no more than the quaver beat of the music and possibly a little slower. When you come to a 'hairpin' *crescendo* mark in the score, stop playing and let the natural swell of the instrument play the *crescendo*. Don't start playing again until the 'hairpin' of the *diminuendo* finishes, then resume beating and start increasing the energy to raise the volume. Carry on like this until the penultimate two *crescendos* where you just need to play the *crescendo* to ensure there is enough energy to give you the volume, then really go for it for the final *fff* and then let it vibrate! Don't dampen it for at least five bars.

8.1.5 Damping

Damping or muffling is a way of suppressing the sound of the tam-tam as these instruments will resonate for a long time if permitted. Damping can range from just touching the tam-tam with the fingers to complete suppression of a loud note using the beater, hands and body! Knowledge of the music score is key to deciding how severe the damping should be as well as knowing how much effort is needed to stop the instrument resonating. A large tam-tam takes some effort to stop whereas a small tam-tam is much easier to control, something that is worth remembering. When playing the 'The Rite of Spring' I use two tam-tams, and use the smaller of the two for the short *crescendo* 'roars' near the end of the first movement. Some may say this is cheating, but you don't need the deep resonant note of a large tam-tam at this point, just the rush of the higher partials.

Whatever the technique used to damp the instrument, be aware that there will be an obvious drop in volume as soon as anything touches the surface of the gong, so an arsenal of damping techniques is required. Take, for instance, the loud tam-tam stroke in the fourth movement of Tchaikovsky's Symphony No.2. If you let it just ring, you'll be there for a very long time and get impatient looks from the conductor and audience. Damp it too quickly with the wrong technique and it will sound musically naff.

Light damping techniques start with the finger(s) on the edge of the tam-tam. For more damping, place the fingers on the face of the instrument or the mallet on the centre front face. More damping can be obtained with a cloth in one hand which then grips the rim of the tam-tam. This last technique is good for controlling volume if the score calls for a series of repeated quiet strokes but you don't want the volume to build up e.g. Respighi's *Pines of Rome* – 4th Movement. For more immediate damping effects try a mallet moved around the face of the gong, or a mallet on the front face and hand on the rear face (preferably with a cloth to avoid finger marks), or a mallet and hands moving around both faces of the tam-tam. For the full emergency stop – press the mallet on the front face and hand on the rear face, pushing the front face of the tam-tam against your legs and thigh.

8.1.6 Tuned Gong Playing

Tuned gongs are rarely played loud as this goes very much against the character of the instrument. Best results are obtained by using softer mallets and you strike the boss of the gong to get a purer tone or the face between the boss and edge for a less clear tone. Unlike tam-tams, you are allowed to strike the centre of the gong as it has been designed to be played in this way. The rolls and damping techniques are equally valid when playing tuned gongs.

8.2   SOUND HEALING PLAYING TECHNIQUES

Playing the gong for sound healing, yoga, other alternative therapies, or for gong concerts or gong pujas is very different to playing the gong in an orchestra or band. For a start, you face the gong and have your back to the audience, so your focus becomes the gong. It is also a much freer style of playing, often involving playing the front, back and edge of the gong with a variety of mallets and beaters, and letting the gong play you rather than you playing the gong. I much prefer this style of playing the gong, but after 25 years of orchestral playing, it took a few lessons to 'loosen up' to this freestyle method. That said, some orchestral techniques can still be used in the sound healing world and vice-versa.

8.2.1 Basic Stroke

Because you are standing up (or sitting down) and facing the gong, which will normally be at chest height, the basic stroke, which still consists of a bounced or glanced blow, tends to be either a downward stroke, glancing off the gong and continuing downwards (in other words, you follow through with the arm and wrist) or a downward stroke bouncing (or ricocheting) back upwards, where the wrist flicks the mallet at the point of contact and the arm pulls the mallet away.

8.2.2 Drone

An important technique in sound healing, the drone forms the basic 'sound' upon which the sound healing therapy is built. Here you beat the gong in the same spot, or at different spots, around the 5 to 7 o'clock position to form a continuous sound. It is normal to start quietly and reach a sustained low volume. Beating faster or harder with the mallet puts more energy into the gong and the volume rises, at which point you can maintain the volume by easing off the strength or number of beats. Often it is good to let the sound decay periodically before bringing up the volume again.

On top of the basic drone other sounds can be made, such as introducing a harder beater to accent the sound, or using another beater to strike different points of the gong to introduce different sounds and timbres. Keeping the drone constant takes some practice. It is easy to lose the energy, especially by self damping with the beaters, or to let the volume rise uncontrollably by putting in too much energy.

8.2.3 Tsunami

The tsunami is a continuation of the drone, except that the energy and the sound is allowed to increase to a point where the higher partials rush out of the gong and crash into the surrounding area like waves crashing onto a rocky shore. The volume is allowed to reach *fortissimo* levels, but there is no real need to go above 50% of what the gong is capable of. Again, enjoy the decaying sound of the gong rather than carrying on at full dynamics.

8.2.4 Heartbeat

A technique produced by using one or two mallets to replicate the beat of the human heart. Different pulses can be used, especially at the start of a healing session where an anxious client can be calmed by reducing the rate of the pulse over a short time period.

8.2.5 Clock Face

This is a technique where the player goes round the face of the gong in either a clockwise or anticlockwise direction, striking the gong at the one, two, three o'clock positions etc. You will be surprised at the number of different sounds that can be produced. Also try experimenting by striking at the two and eight o'clock position, or the ten and four o'clock positions or my particular favourite, the three, six, nine and twelve o'clock positions.

8.2.6 Swinging Door

Based on the preceding method, strike the gong at the three and nine o'clock positions to set the gong swinging from side to side. The gong will do this at its own rate, pivoting about the support hooks like the doors on a Wild West saloon bar. Don't try and force the rate of swing, as you invariably end up striking the gong as it swings towards you, thereby damping the swinging effect. A difficult technique to master, the trick is to strike the gong as the side moves away from you. The effect is used to balance the left and right hemispheres of the brain. A word of warning though – check the gong cord to make sure it is in good condition before attempting this and don't do it if the gong is supported on a gallows-type stand.

8.2.7 Pendulum

This technique involves getting the gong to swing fore and aft. Strike the gong at the six o'clock position, giving it a slight push away from you as you strike it with the beater. To keep it swinging, strike the gong as it moves away from you – if you strike it as it comes towards you the gong will stop in its tracks and damp the sound. The audible effect is a slight Doppler sound as the gong swings back and forth. Again, check the hanging cord and don't do this with a gallows type stand, or some floor mounted stands with small feet, as the stand may topple over.

8.2.8 Thunderclap

This is a *fortissimo* stroke designed to bring out a loud crash in the middle of your playing. Strike at the sweet spot using a heavy glancing blow. An effective way to do this is to stand to the side of the gong, stretch out your arm and strike the gong in an upward or downward movement with an accompanying flick of the wrist. Use sparingly!

8.2.9 Slurs and Ties

Some gong practitioners make use of a couple of musical terms in their description of playing techniques. The 'tie' is where two musical notes of the same pitch are 'tied' together to produce a longer note than the time value of the individual notes would normally allow. The 'slur' is the same effect between two different pitched notes. In percussion terms, 'ties' are produced by rolls of the sticks for the correct length of time, or letting the instrument vibrate for the appropriate time, without sounding the second note. In effect you just hear one note being produced. 'Slurs' only occur with pitched instruments such as the xylophone or timpani. In gong playing terms, what you are actually doing is either striking the same spot twice (tie) or striking two different spots (slur). Personally, it doesn't justify the use of these terms to describe these techniques, they are just individual notes at the same or different parts of the gong.

8.2.10 Flams, Drags and Ruffs

Some percussion rudiments that can be used in gong playing are 'Flams' and 'Drags'. A 'Flam' is where one grace note precedes the main note and can be produced by using two mallets in quick succession, or by a quick double beat using one mallet. Use of a smaller, harder mallet in the two-mallet technique gives a certain edge or clarity to the grace note.

A 'drag' is where two grace notes precede the main note and can be produced by alternating rapidly between two mallets, one in each hand, or using three mallets, two of which are in one hand, preferably smaller than the main beater, and 'rocking' them quickly for the two beats before the main stroke.

A 'ruff' is where three grace notes precede the main note and is pretty useless for gong playing as the sound gets too mushy.

8.2.11 Muffling and Damping

The techniques for muffling and damping the gong described in the orchestral techniques Section are equally valid here, though the range of techniques is somewhat more limited. They are usually confined to placing the mallet on the gong either just off centre or moving the mallet around the face of the gong, or by grabbing the edge of the gong. In most cases, damping is not used during a session as the natural decay of the gong sound is part of the overall treatment and damping can appear quite abrupt.

8.3   WALKING GONG TECHNIQUES

Rarely used in an orchestral or band context, 'walking gongs' (i.e. wandering around the room or venue with a gong) is a commonly used technique in sound healing. The main use for a gong in this way is for 'space clearing' – moving negative or bad energy around to dissipate it. Walking gong techniques can also be used to focus energy on an individual, by moving a gong over a particular part of the body. I use tuned gongs in this way, focussing on a particular area of the body or Chakra.

Small gongs tend to be used for walking techniques, often 20"/50cm to 24"/60cm in diameter. Larger sizes are occasionally used by people with good arm strength, but the gong can become unwieldy due to its size and diameter, rather than just because of the weight. I find that the 24" Wuhan Chao gong, 24"/60cm Paiste Symphonic and Planet gongs are good for this technique. The ideal gongs are 'Wind' gongs, as the higher partials can easily be sounded without too much effort on the part of the player, and are much lighter to carry.

In all cases, the condition of the gut or cord supporting the gong, plus the security of the knots are of paramount importance. The last thing you want is a cord snapping, or a knot giving way or you losing your grip on the gong. At best, the gong will hit the floor or other inanimate object, damaging itself. At worst, it will hit a person with a very good chance of severely injuring them.

The technique involves holding the gong cord in one hand and striking it with a beater in the other, and moving the gong around in certain ways. These include:-

The Fan – wafting the gong backwards and forwards

The Pendulum – swinging the gong from side to side

The Spin – twirling the gong on its cord

The Lift – moving the gong up and down in a vertical fashion

The Shake – shaking the gong

There are a couple of other techniques that you may come across. The *Whirling Dervish* is a technique where the struck gong is held at arms length as you spin on the spot. The *Healing Vortex* involves moving the gong in a vertical circle above and behind your head, striking it on the downward pass. Both these techniques, in my opinion, a high risk of injury to both gong and player, have no real place in sound healing, and are little more than showmanship.

8.4   EXPERIMENT

The techniques described in this Section are just general pointers to help you play the gong. You need to develop your own style of playing and explore what works for you, what works for the passage of music or the composer's intention, and what sounds you are trying to achieve. Above all, experiment! Try different ways of striking the gong, different beaters, flumi and mallets, your position in relation to the gong, and playing on different parts of the gong. Have fun!

REFERENCES – CHAPTER 8

1.   Benton, Mehta, *Gong Yoga – Healing and Enlightenment Through Sound*, iUniverse, 2008

2.   Whittaker, Sheila, *Sound Healing with Gongs – A Gong Book for Beginners* Healing Sound, 2010

3.   www.vicfirth.com/education/percussion101-concertGong.php

APPENDIX A – Resources

GONG MANUFACTURERS/BRANDED GONG DISTRIBUTORS

Paiste

Paiste GmbH & Co. Gorch-Fock-Str 13, D-24790, Schacht Audorf, Germany.

www.paiste.com

UFIP (Unione Fabbricanti Italiani Piatti)

s.r.l Via Galileo, 20 1-51100, Pistoia, Italy

www.ufip.it

Sabian

219 Main St, Meductic, New Brunswick, Canada, E6H 2L5

www.sabian.com

Zildjian

Avedis Zildjian Co. 22 Longwater Drive, Norwell, MA 02061, USA

www.zildjian.com

Wuhan China Golden Bird

Wuhan China Golden Bird Fine Gong Manufacture Co. Ltd, Xiajiazui, Xintian, Caidian District, Wuhan, Hubei 430101, China

www.chinawuhangong.com

Wuhan Haiping

Wuhan Haiping Musical Instruments Manufacture Co. Ltd.

230 Gan Tang Road, Huangpi, Wuhan, China. 430334

www.chinagong.com

www.eastgong.com

Roland Meinl Musikinstrumente GmbH & Co Kg

An Den Herrenbergen 24, D-91413 Neustadt/Aisch,

Germany

www.meinldistribution.eu/.com

Dream Cymbals and Gongs

www.dreamcymbals.com

Stagg Music

Stagg Music, c/o EMD Music

16a Boulevard General Wahis, Schaerbeek 1030

Brussels, Belgium

www.staggmusic.com

Percussion Plus

Unit F, Welland Business Park, Valley Way, Market Harborough,
Leics. LC16 7PG

www.percussionplus.co.uk

GONG STOCKISTS AND DEALERS – UK

eCymbals

19 Cheapside, Liverpool, Merseyside, England. L2 2DY, England

www.ecymbals.co.uk

JAM Percussion Ltd

8 Dakota Business Park, Skyhawk Avenue, Liverpool, England, L19 2QR

www.jampercussion.com

Bell Percussion Ltd

6 Greenock Road, London W3 8DU

www.bellperc.com

Cymbal Centre (UFIP distributor)

56 Atholl Street, Perth, Scotland, PH1 5NL

www.cymbalcentre.co.uk

Sound Travels

Brookfield Farm, Prestbury, Cheltenham, Gloucestershire GL52 3NQ

www.soundtravels.co.uk

Soul Notes

P.O. Box 88, Dawlish, Devon, EX7 0WG

www.soulnote.co.uk

GONG STOCKISTS AND DEALERS – USA

Gongs Unlimited

1143 Mulder Drive, Lincoln, Nebraska 68510, USA.

www.gongs-unlimited.com

Memphis Gong Chamber

878 S Cooper Street, Memphis, Tennessee 38104

www.memphisgongchamber.com

Artdrum

Hopewell, New Jersey 08525

www.artdrum.com

STANDS, BEATERS, STICKS AND MALLETS, CASE AND BAG MAKERS

Most good percussion and drum shops stock some or many of the above products described in this book. Apart from Chalklin who do not have a website at present, I have just listed the websites of the various manufacturers for information.

Chalklin Percussion, PD Chalklin, Southern Cross, The Ridgeway, Chiseldon, Wiltshire, SN4 0HT, England.

www.humes-berg.com

www.jampercussion.com

www.leblond.co.uk

www.protectionracket.co.uk

www.sabian.com

www.vicfirth.com

www.mikebalter.com

www.ukyamaha.com

www.paiste.com

www.ufip.it

APPENDIX B – Gongs in Classical Music

In this Section I have listed a number of pieces of classical music which feature the tam-tam or gong prominently, extensively or in a particular way. This list does not include every piece of classical music that uses either instrument, as it is questionable what the purpose of such a list would be. Also, in many pieces the tam-tam or gong may only appear once, or may be played in such a way that, to be quite honest, one questions the purpose of including it at all!

In Chapter 8 I made a challenge to professional percussion players and it also applies here with regard to recording engineers, mixing editors, and the extent to which conductors are involved in the production process. Recording microphones are not usually placed near the tam-tam due to the perceived volume that it could produce during the piece. While this may be relevant for *fortissimo* strokes, *piano* strokes often go unnoticed whilst listening to the recording. Having said that, there are also occasions where even *fortissimo* strokes either cannot be heard or are barely heard, which means that for the tam-tam lover, a great orchestra/ conductor combination doesn't necessarily ensure a good recording of the percussion section. A classic example of this is the ending of Ravel's orchestration of Mussorgsky's *Pictures at an Exhibition* where several loud strokes on the tam-tam replicate the bell above the Great Gate of Kiev. I am astounded at the number of recordings where you can barely hear this important effect which is scored *fortissimo* ! Fortunately there is at least one recording where this isn't a problem. Hence this list also includes suggestions of certain recordings where the gong or tam-tam can readily be heard, or where the instrument being played has been recorded particularly well.

Although this list is about classical music (and I use this term in its overarching genre meaning) I have also indulged myself with a few film scores where there has been some distinctive scoring for tam-tam, and one score which includes practically every playing style and effect you can get from this instrument. Finally, this is a personal list and very subjective so I expect some of you to disagree with me. In which case, send me your recommendations!

Arnold, Malcolm

Symphonies Nos. 1, 2, 4, 5, 7, 8

Tam O'Shanter Overture

Concerto for 2 Pianos

Peterloo Overture

English Dances

The tam-tam figures extensively throughout Arnold's music, particularly in his symphonies. There are several good recordings of Arnold's music, but for me the recordings of the symphonies with Richard Hickox and the London Symphony Orchestra and Rumon Gamba with the BBC Philharmonic on the Chandos label are hard to beat. The tam-tam stroke in the third movement of the Symphony No.2 is sublime and probably one of the best recordings of a tam-tam stroke anywhere.

Bax, Arnold

Symphonies Nos.1 and 4

A tam-tam stroke underpins the climax of the slow movement of the Symphony No.1and the angst in this work takes Bax another six symphonies to resolve.

Berlioz, Hector

Requiem

Seen by many as the father of percussion, Berlioz was a keen experimenter with percussion, especially multiple examples of one instrument. His Requiem is possibly his most extravagant – six sets of timpani, ten cymbals and three tam-tams! Although this seems excessive, probably the poor quality of the instruments compared to those of today was the reason for using so many. When performed today with the same numbers it can be quite spectacular. The combined *fortissimo* crash of all the cymbals and tam-tams in the Tuba Mirum is like a bomb going off! In the recording by EMI of Andre Previn and the London Philharmonic, it is positively thermo-nuclear!

Boulez, Pierre
Rituel; In Memorium Bruno Maderna

Well known as a conductor and champion of modern classical music and *avante-garde* works, Boulez is also a composer. In his *Rituel* he uses both tuned gongs (seven) and tam-tams. I first heard this piece at a BBC Prom Concert where the BBC Symphony Orchestra used Paiste tuned gongs and tam-tams. The recording by Sony Classical using the same forces several years later however, finds the tuned gongs replaced by Burmese tuned gongs. During the *piano* sections they're fine, when played loudly they sound dreadful!

Brian, Havergal
Symphony No.1 'Gothic'
Symphonies No. 3, 7 and 9 plus several others

The forgotten British composer, overshadowed by his monumental 'Gothic' Symphony (requiring huge orchestral forces), wrote 32 symphonies as well as operas and other orchestral works. The tam-tam (though Brian calls it a gong) is used in many of his pieces, though somewhat sparingly. There is a passage in the last movement of the 'Gothic' where it performs almost a duet with the bass soloist. Also, several of the symphonies (e.g. Nos.7,and 8) end with a Brian trademark – a *pianissimo* stroke on the tam-tam.

Brittain, Benjamin

'Four Sea Interludes' from *Peter Grimes*

War Requiem

'Passacaglia'

Young Person's Guide to the Orchestra

Saint Nicholas

The tam-tam (or gong as Britten refers to it) features in a number of works by Benjamin Britten. In the 'Four Sea Interludes' it plays both the part of a bell and a crash of thunder in the 'Storm'. There is a prominent role for it in the War Requiem and the recording by EMI featuring The City of Birmingham Symphony Orchestra conducted by Simon Rattle is particularly good in this respect. It is also one of the rare occasions where a Wuhan Chao gong is being used by a British orchestra.

Copland, Aaron

'Fanfare for the Common Man'

Symphony No. 3

Essentially the same piece of music in two different forms, the 'Fanfare for the Common Man' is instantly recognisable. The piece works well with either Paiste or Chao tam-tams, though in some recordings with North American orchestras the large Wuhan Chao tam-tams used can be a little too dark. Copland scored the fanfare in his Symphony No. 3 at the beginning of the fourth movement and returning in a blaze of glory at the end. HMV's recording with the Dallas Symphony Orchestra under Eduardo Mata features a particularly fine Wuhan Chao tam-tam.

Debussy, Claude

La Mer

Much has been written about Debussy's fascination with an Indonesian gamelan heard at the Paris Exposition in 1889 but little direct replication of the gamelan style found its way into his music. Certainly he didn't score for various gongs in any of his pieces and even the tam-tam is rare. It is, however, used to great effect in *La Mer*, especially in the final movement – 'Dialogue between the Wind and the Waves'.

Elgar, Edward

The Dream of Gerontius

The March of the Mogul Emperors (*Crown of India Suite*)

The tam-tam (or gong as Elgar refers to it) appears rarely in his works. In fact, Elgar was pretty light on the use of percussion in most of his works except for the marches. And it is to one of these marches that we turn for one of my favourite uses of the tam-tam – 'The March of the Mogul Emperors' from the *Crown of India Suite*. An unashamedly brash and imperial piece of music, the piece ends with loud strokes as the procession lines up in front of Edward VII. A recommended recording is the Deutsches Grammophon version with Leonard Bernstein conducting the BBC Symphony Orchestra. This was a 'filler' piece for his astonishing recording of the *Enigma Variations* (the very slow rendition of 'Nimrod' vociferously splitting opinion) and was done in just one take!

Gershwin, George

Rhapsody in Blue

Piano Concerto in F

Although used a couple of times in *Rhapsody in Blue*, the real gem is the single loud stroke towards the end of the Piano Concerto in F – one of the classic uses of the tam-tam, rounding off a passage of music before the next section follows. It is almost as though energy is being dissipated following a furious or intense preceding passage. Other examples include Tchaikovsky Symphony No.2 and certain versions of Rachmaninov's Symphony No. 1. Both Paiste and Wuhan tam-tams work well with this piece but it should be played loudly and without hesitation.

Holst, Gustav

The Planets Suite

Beni Mora

The tam-tam is used extensively in 'Mars' but also makes an appearance in 'Uranus' plus a *piano* stroke in 'Neptune'. For me, the piece only works when a Paiste tam-tam is used. The classic recording is Sir Adrian Boult and the London Philharmonic on the EMI label. The use of the tam-tam in *Beni Mora* is another classic energy dissipation scoring.

Hovhanness, Alan

Symphony No. 50 'Mount St. Helens'

A prolific writer of symphonies and other orchestral works, Hovhanness in his Symphony No.50 depicts the eruption of Mount St. Helens. There is a prolific use of the tam-tam in the third movement and a significant part for the timpani as well. The recording by the Royal Liverpool Philharmonic Orchestra under Gerard Schwarz on Telarc is particularly good and uses a Wuhan tam-tam rather than the normal Paiste instrument.

Khachaturian, Aram

Symphony No.2 'The Bell'

Spartacus – Adagio

Although featuring in a number of his works, the tam-tam is given a good workout in the third movement of his Second Symphony. I have only come across Soviet recordings of the symphony and in both cases, Wuhan tam-tams are used. The recording with Khachaturian himself conducting the Armenian Philharmonic Orchestra probably has the edge over his other recording with the USSR Symphony. The tam-tam has a little more depth and size.

Lloyd, George

Symphony No.6

Symphony No.11

Another of our 'forgotten' British composers, George Lloyd bucked the *avante garde* movement amongst British composers (such as Maxwell Davis, Oliver Knussen and others) and wrote music that was very easy to listen to. Percussion, apart from timpani, is rare in his music and tends to be used sparingly like Elgar did. His Symphony No. 11 is a riot of percussion though, and has a prominent role for the tam-tam. Listen for it after the brass fanfare at the start of the fourth movement but don't have the volume too high! Lloyd's recording with the Albany Symphony Orchestra on the Conifer label is about the only version available and features that rare beast – an American orchestra using a Paiste tam-tam!

Mahler, Gustav

Symphonies Nos. 1 – 9

Das Lied von der Erde

All the Mahler symphonies feature the tam-tam and Symphony No. 2 has the luxury of two of them (high and low). They are used in a variety of ways from cataclysmic crashes to tolling *piano* strokes in the various death marches to terrifying *crescendos*. The final movement of '*Das Lied von der Erde*' is almost a dialogue between tam-tam and the *mezzo-soprano* soloist, and Symphony No. 2 features a particularly difficult to control rhythmic section in the final movement. Both Chao and Paiste tam-tams work well in all performances *except* for the endings of Symphonies No. 2 and 8 where only a Paiste tam-tam (and a large one at that) will do. This is because the Paiste tam-tams have better sustaining power at loud volumes, and the endings of these symphonies require an explosion of higher frequency sound that shouldn't decay away instantly. There are a few excellent interpreters of Mahler symphonies – Haitink, Bernstein and Maazel to name three – but for me it is Klaus Tennstedt and the London Symphony Orchestra on EMI for the recommended discs, and Wyn Morris and the Symphonica of London (for a slightly tidier ending) to Symphony No.8.

Messiaen, Olivier

Turangalila Symphonie

Des Canyons aux Etoiles

Coleurs de la Cite Celeste

La Transfiguration de Notre Seigneur Jesus Christ

Et Exspecto Resurrectionem Mortuorem

Oiseaux Exotiques

For me, Messiaen is 'Mr Gong' when it comes to their use in orchestral music. His use of percussion and his rhythmic transcription of bird song and Eastern songs and rhythms makes for exciting, if sometimes difficult, music to listen to. Messiaen uses both gongs and tam-tams, often using multiples of each instrument. Turangalila only uses one tam-tam, though Simon Rattle's performance with The City of Birmingham Symphony uses both Paiste and Wuhan Chao tam-tams and makes an interesting 'spot the difference' recording. *Des Canyons* uses four gongs and tam-tam, *Et Exspecto* uses a remarkable six gongs and three tam-tams but even this is trumped by *La Transfiguration* which uses seven gongs and three tam-tams. In fact, this work starts with the seven gongs and two of the tam-tams chiming away from small to large, a passage which occurs several times in the work.

The main problem with recordings of Messiaen's music is that, apart from 'Turangalila', there aren't many recordings to choose from and where they exist, the quality of the gongs and tam-tams is not very good. Often, Wuhan Chao tam-tams are used and the small- and medium-sized ones can sound like rubbish bin lids. Paiste tuned gongs are often used but have quite bad metal fatigue in recordings I have heard. For good quality sounding gongs and tam-tams, the recordings of *Coleurs*, *Des Canyons* and *Oiseaux* by the London Sinfonietta under Esa-Pekka Salonen on Sony is a must. *Et Exspecto* has some dreadful tam-tams being used in some recordings and the recording by the Berlin Radio Symphony Orchestra under Karl Anton Rickenbacher is about the best that has been available to date, though some of the gongs and the small tam-tam are not brilliant quality. Their recording of *La Transfiguration* is very good though, with larger tam-tams being used, especially the largest of the three which is a beautifully deep Wuhan Chao instrument.

Orff, Carl

Carmina Burana

Whenever I have played this piece, there is usually a fight amongst the percussionists to play the tam-tam part. Probably one of the best known parts for tam-tam and one of the most satisfying to play, this work uses it for great effect in 'O Fortuna' at the beginning and end of the work. If you have a recording where you can't hear the tam-tam, ask for your money back and demand the resignation of the percussionist or recording engineer. In my opinion, you play it loud and without mercy!

Prokofiev, Sergei

Symphony No. 5

Although used in other works, it is the use of the tam-tam in the first movement of the Symphony No. 5 (and again in the third movement) that sets this apart from his other works. This movement is dark and brooding, moving towards a threatening climax that is punctuated with several *fortissimo* strokes on the tam-tam. By now, most readers have probably noticed that I have a slight leaning towards the Paiste tam-tams for classical music. Every now and again, however, there comes along a Chao tam-tam that knocks the Paiste version into a cocked hat. Such an instrument can be found in the recording of this work by the St. Louis Symphony Orchestra under the direction of Leonard Slatkin on the RCA Victor label. No attempt has been made by the recording crew or the player to balance this bit with the rest of the orchestra – it is very much 'in your face'. The instrument has a reasonable sustain to it as well as some 'guts' that is just right for this piece.

Rachmaninov, Sergei

Symphony No. 1

Symphonic Dances

The Symphony No. 1 is one of those pieces that, in my view, justifies a bit of artistic licence on behalf of the conductor. There are four loud tam-tam strokes at the end of the symphony, but it is the one towards the end of the fast passage in the fourth movement, where the music comes to an abrupt stop, that is the issue. In the score, this passage stops suddenly with a short final note from the orchestra on the last beat of the bar. The tam-tam is scored to play on the first beat of the following bar and *mezzo piano*. The effect is that all this energy from the orchestra comes to an abrupt halt with nowhere to go and is poorly dealt with by a wimpish stroke on the tam-tam. There are several recordings like this, with varying loudness of the tam-tam, but it is the single beat gap that spoils the effect and leaves you feeling somewhat deflated. Some conductors have felt the same as I do and such a person is Edo de Waart with his recording of this symphony on Phillips with the Rotterdam Philharmonic. Here, he shifts the tam-tam stroke to the end of the previous bar and scores it *fortissimo*. The effect immediately dissipates the wild energy of the orchestra in this passage, somewhat akin to a car spinning wildly out of control, hitting a brick wall and exploding into flames!

Another piece that is also open to the whim of the conductor is the *Symphonic Dances*. This was Rachmaninov's last orchestral work and it makes judicious use of the tam-tam in the final pages, using both long strokes and *staccato* strokes in the run to the end of the piece. The final stroke is actually meant to be left to vibrate whilst the rest of the orchestra has stopped. In reality, many performances actually damp this final stroke. This way gives a definite ending to the piece, but I do like the *laisser vibrer* (leave to vibrate) ending, both to hear the wonderful sound of a tam-tam played loudly and to smile wryly at those members of the audience who start to applaud thinking that the piece has ended with the final *staccato* orchestra chords.

Ravel/Mussorgsky

Pictures at an Exhibition

There have been several orchestrations of Mussorgsky's original work for piano, but Ravel's version is perhaps the best known. The last movement – The Great Gate of Kiev – has a very prominent part for the tam-tam, supported by an Eb bell, depicting the large bell that sat on top of the gate in question. Immensely satisfying to play (should be *fortissimo*) but very frustrating to listen to as in many recordings you can hardly hear the tam-tam. About the only recording that has it recorded with the right prominence is EMI's recording with the Philadelphia Orchestra conducted by Riccardo Muti. Simon Rattle and the Berlin Philharmonic is a close second, but the BPO's Chao tam-tam is a tad too dark for this work.

Respighi, Ottorino

Pines of Rome
Roman Festivals
Church Windows
Symphonia Drammatica

Respighi uses the tam-tam in quite spectacular fashion in many of his works. This is a mark of the quality of the Italian gong and tam-tam makers that eventually joined together to form UFIP. In *Pines of Rome*, the tam-tam is used in 'bell' mode in the second movement representing a religious plain chant section. In the final movement it is used to punctuate the depiction of a Roman army marching up the Apian Way with a variety of crescendo rolls, staccato barks and full-blown crashes. In *Roman Festivals* the tam-tam is used in a series of short strokes representing the growls of lions prowling around the unfortunate Christians in the Circus Maximus. *Church Windows* uses three tam-tams of different sizes in a lovely chiming motif in the final movement but is best remembered for the *fortississimo* crash at the end of 'St Michael, Archangel' as Satan is banished from heaven. Finally, in a manner reminiscent of the Roman army section of *Pines of Rome*, there is a wonderful section in the first movement of the *Symphonia Drammatica*. The music starts quietly with a stately theme, gradually building up in intensity. The tam-tam suddenly appears from the music in a dramatic *crescendo* roll reaching *fortississimo* as the music reaches a climax before loud crashes toll out, gradually dying away in intensity as the music fades at the same time.

Although the Roman triptych is usually issued as a compilation on one CD, this does not necessarily mean that all three recordings are the best available of all three works. *Pines of Rome* suffers from poor recording or underplaying of the tam-tam in many versions. In Lorin Maazel's recording with the Pittsburg Symphony on Sony Classical the tam-tam is very distinct but in *Roman Festival* on the same disk, it is quite inaudible in many sections. Conversely Seigi Ozawa and the Boston Symphony on DG has a quite inaudible tam-tam in *Pines of Rome* but a very forceful one in *Roman Festivals*. Geoffrey Simon and the Philharmonia on Chandos has the best crash at the end of the second movement of *Church Windows* as all three instruments are used at once, and the tam-tam used by the BBC Philharmonic under Ted Downes on the Chandos label in its recording of *Sinfonia Dramattica* is a top quality Paiste Symphonic Gong very much at the start of its playing career.

Rimsky-Korsakov, Nikolai

Scheherazade

Russian Easter Festival Overture

There is a straightforward tam-tam crash in the last movement of *Scheherazade* which represents Sinbad's ship crashing onto the rocks. Scored *forte* in the music parts, I always feel that playing it *fortissimo* has a better effect. In the Russian Easter Festival Overture, the composer calls for the tam-tam to be played *quasi-campana* or 'like a bell'. This is an interesting challenge for the player which involves using more of the fundamental note and controlling the higher overtones. Hence a larger tam-tam is often required, or experiment with striking at different points on the face of the instrument, or using different types of mallet.

Shostakovich, Dmitri

Symphonies

The tam-tam is used in all the symphonies except Nos. 9 and 14. It is used in a variety of ways – thundering crashes, quiet chiming, threatening *mezzo fortes*. There are many interesting passages to listen to – try the last movement of Symphony No. 4, two loud crashes in a maelstrom of sound, the first movement of Symphony No.6 with a single *piano* stroke supporting menacing bass strings and woodwind; and the third movement of Symphony No. 8 where it replicates shell explosions. Also Symphony No. 12 where it is used in every mode, Symphony No. 13 in the first movement in a harrowing portrayal of the executions at Babi Yar and Symphony No. 15 at the end of the climax of the last movement. But if I was to choose one symphony to illustrate the use of the tam-tam by Shostakovich it would have to be Symphony No. 11. Loud crashes and *piano* strokes abound throughout the symphony but the musical portrayal of the massacre of peasants in front of the Winter Palace in 1904 is a classic piece of sound painting. The tam-tam is employed here to portray the rifle volleys delivered by the Imperial Guard and hence should be played in normal fashion as long crashes left to vibrate. It should not be played using a metal beater scraped over the surface as in some recordings. The recording by the London Symphony Orchestra under Rostropovich is one of the better recordings, though this section is a little slow compared to a live version I attended with the same forces two years before this recording. On balance, I believe a Paiste tam-tam works better with the Shostakovich symphonies, but the Chao tam-tam occasionally used by the Royal Liverpool Philharmonic Orchestra in the Schwartz and Petrenko recordings shows that this is not always the case.

Stockhausen, Karlheinz

Mikrophonie 1

Two players, two microphones, a table full of beaters, scrapers and other odds and sods and a 60-inch tam-tam. Have fun!

Strauss, Richard

Death and Transfiguration

'Alpine' Symphony

A classic use of the tam-tam in funereal mode, the quiet chimes in *Death and Transfiguration* take the music of Strauss from one world to the next and set us up for one of the most moving passages of music ever written. A deep Chao tam-tam really works well here. In the 'Alpine' Symphony, the tam-tam in one passage takes on the role of thunder and lightning in the storm, ably supported by the thunder machine and lightning sheet.

Stravinsky, Igor

The Rite of Spring

A definitive tam-tam role discussed at various points in this book so I won't comment further. Chao tam-tams work better here due to their ability to 'speak' faster than the Paiste equivalent. There are many recordings but my recommendation is Riccardo Muti and the Philadelphia Orchestra as it is a decent effort and comes with the recommended version of Ravel/ Mussorgsky *Pictures at an Exhibition*. Bit of a gong fest CD!

Tchaikovsky, Petr Il'ich

Symphonies Nos. 2 and 6

Tone Poem 'Manfred'

'Marche Slave'

Francesca da Rimini

Swan Lake (finale)

A first glance, Tchaikovsky's works are not the sort of pieces where one would expect to find tam-tams. But, as you can see from the list, they are used quite frequently. The most famous use is the single stroke in the last movement of the Symphony No. 6. Another 'fate' stroke, it is actually scored *mezzo piano* but most recordings have a somewhat pathetic (note – not 'pathetique' which is the sub-title of the symphony) *pianissimo* stroke.

The aim is to get a full sound of the fundamental note with little higher overtones, hence a large tam-tam is needed. Conversely, the loud crash at the end of the fast passage in the fourth movement of the Symphony No. 2 needs to be full sounding with plenty of crash, but not damped too soon nor allowed to carry on vibrating (which could result in the rest of the orchestra going for a cup of tea!). There are many other excellent passages for the tam-tam (especially the end of *Francesca da Rimini*) but for me, the ending of *Swan Lake* takes some beating, especially in the recording by Charles Dutoit and the Montreal Symphony Orchestra.

Tippett, Michael

Triple Concerto

No tam-tams in this work but six different-sized tuned gongs are used to recall the gamelan sound Tippett had heard at one time. The recording by the Bournemouth Symphony Orchestra under Richard Hickox is about one of the only ones available The Paiste tuned gongs are only just audible but when they do appear they do give an exotic feel to the music.

Vaughn Williams, Ralph

Symphonies No. 2, No. 7 & No. 8

Job – A Masque for Dancing

There is a quite spectacular crash on a tam-tam heralding the arrival of the organ in 'Sinfonia Antartica' (Symphony No. 7) but also representing blocks of ice crashing into the sea, and Symphony No. 8 uses both tuned gongs and a tam-tam as well as every 'phone' and 'speil' known to man! The Symphony No. 2 only has the one note, played at the climax of the last movement and in many ways is nothing spectacular. But the recording of the one used by the Halle Orchestra under Sir John Barbirolli (EMI) deserves special mention. Recorded in 1967, I think this is one of the earliest recordings of the current version of the Paiste Symphonic Gong. The recording is beautifully balanced and the tam-tam has a lovely re-sound and sustain.

Walton, William

Symphony No. 1

Belshazzar's Feast

'Crown Imperial'

There is a great part for tam-tam at the end of the Symphony No. 1 which makes an appearance with the second set of timpani and the cymbals. It is scored *forte* and as a result it can suffer from being underplayed both in live performances and recordings. It is not meant to be brash but still audible. Leonard Slatkin and the London Philharmonic on Virgin Records get pretty close to what it should sound like. There is a recording made in the 1950s with Walton conducting one English orchestra which should be avoided. The tam-tam is dreadful – the proverbial dustbin lid!

Belshazzar's Feast has a great section in it where the pagan gods of gold, silver, iron, wood and brass are praised by the choir and includes representations of each metal in the percussion. Iron is represented by the anvil and a strike on the tam-tam with a metal stick. The tam-tam also is also used in a threatening series of *pianissimo* strokes during the appearance of God's finger at the climax of the feast writing out Belshazzar's doom with the words 'You have been weighed in the balance and found wanting,' and then in a series of triumphant crashes during the final 'Sing Aloud' celebration by the freed slaves. Unfortunately, this last series of crashes often gets drowned out in both live and recorded performances, and I have yet to find a recording where it can be heard clearly.

Barry, John

James Bond Film Scores

The tam-tam is used widely throughout the film scores, especially in the various versions of the theme tune where several different tam-tams are used depending on the band. It is used extensively in *You Only Live Twice* and *The Man with the Golden Gun* because of their Far East settings.

Elfman, Danny

Batman

A dark score for a dark film. The original motion picture score uses a particularly nice Wuhan Chao tam-tam, which also appears in other scores. I'm not sure of the name of the orchestra beyond 'a studio orchestra'.

Shore, Howard

Lord of the Rings

These three scores are a consummate lesson in composing for, playing, and recording of the tam-tam in just about every conceivable way. The original motion picture soundtrack was recorded with the London Philharmonic Orchestra which uses a particularly pleasing Paiste Symphonic Gong.